RELIGIOUS DIVE

Philosophical and Political Dimensions

Should we merely celebrate diversity in the sphere of religion? What of the social cohesion of a country? There is a constant tug-of-war between belief in religious truth and the need for respect for other religions. *Religious Diversity: Philosophical and Political Dimensions* examines how far a firm faith can allow for toleration of difference and respect the need for religious freedom. It elucidates the philosophical credentials of different approaches to truth in religion, ranging from a dogmatic fundamentalism to a pluralism that shades into relativism. Must we resort to a secularism that treats all religion as a personal and private matter, with nothing to contribute to discussions about the common good? How should law approach the issue of religious freedom? Having introduced the relevance of central discussions in modern philosophy of religion, the book goes on to examine the political implications of increasing religious diversity in a democracy.

Roger Trigg is Emeritus Professor of Philosophy at the University of Warwick and Senior Research Fellow at the Ian Ramsey Centre, University of Oxford. He is past President of the European Society for Philosophy of Religion, as well as the British Society for Philosophy of Religion. He is the author of many books in philosophy, particularly in the philosophy of religion and the philosophy of science and social science, including *Reason and Commitment* (Cambridge University Press, 1973), *Religion in Public Life: Must Religion Be Privatized?* (2007), and *Equality, Freedom and Religion* (2012). He has lectured widely in different countries, including Russia, on issues concerning religion in public life and religious freedom. He is currently Associate Scholar at Georgetown University with the Religious Freedom Project at the Berkley Center. He is a member of the Center of Theological Inquiry in Princeton, New Jersey.

Cambridge Studies in Religion, Philosophy, and Society

Series editors:

Paul Moser, *Loyola University Chicago*
Chad Meister, *Bethel College*

This is a series of interdisciplinary texts devoted to major-level courses in religion, philosophy, and related fields. It includes original, current, and wide-spanning contributions by leading scholars from various disciplines that (a) focus on the central academic topics in religion and philosophy; (b) are seminal and up to date regarding recent developments in scholarship on the various key topics; and (c) incorporate, with needed precision and depth, the major differing perspectives and backgrounds – the central voices on the major religions and the religious, philosophical, and sociological viewpoints that cover the intellectual landscape today. Cambridge Studies in Religion, Philosophy, and Society is a direct response to this recent and widespread interest and need.

RELIGIOUS DIVERSITY
Philosophical and Political Dimensions

ROGER TRIGG

The University of Oxford

CAMBRIDGE
UNIVERSITY PRESS

CAMBRIDGE
UNIVERSITY PRESS

32 Avenue of the Americas, New York, NY 10013-2473, USA

Cambridge University Press is part of the University of Cambridge.

It furthers the University's mission by disseminating knowledge in the pursuit of education, learning, and research at the highest international levels of excellence.

www.cambridge.org
Information on this title: www.cambridge.org/9781107638778

© Roger Trigg 2014

First published 2014

Printed in the United States of America

A catalog record for this publication is available from the British Library.

Library of Congress Cataloging in Publication Data
Trigg, Roger.
Religious diversity : philosophical and political dimensions / Roger Trigg.
pages cm. – (Cambridge studies in religion, philosophy, and society)
Includes bibliographical references and index.
ISBN 978-1-107-02360-4 (hardback) – ISBN 978-1-107-63877-8 (pbk.)
1. Freedom of religion. 2. Religious tolerance. 3. Cultural pluralism. I. Title.
BL640.T75 2014
201′.5–dc23   2013042596

ISBN 978-1-107-02360-4 Hardback
ISBN 978-1-107-63877-8 Paperback

For Anna, Nicholas, Lydia, and Clara

CONTENTS

INTRODUCTION

As a result of what sociologists call "globalization," with modern travel and communications, growing economic links, and mass movements of populations from one continent to another, peoples of many different cultures and religions find themselves in daily contact with each other. There have always been many religions, but people have not always been constantly challenged by alternatives. They were able to live in their own small sphere and not have to face real differences from day to day. Settled communities could become very complacent and inward-looking. That has not always been so. The ancient Roman Empire was, for example, awash with different cultures and religions rubbing up against each other. Differing religions have always had to take account of religious diversity, and to be aware of competition.

Even so, in the modern world, no one can escape the fact of diversity in religion and elsewhere, and it is bound to provoke problems in a more pressing way than in previous generations. Two aspects of this are particularly important. Many, both believers and non-believers, can see such diversity and wonder whether the plethora of religions may not cancel the significance of any. They are so different that it appears impossible for them all to be true. The rational conclusion might be that none of them are. Another reaction could be that it is not the function of religion to proclaim "truth." Either way, the self-understanding of different religions is challenged. Major questions in the philosophy of religion have to be confronted. Some, indeed, put the fact of religious diversity in the same category as the vexed problem of evil, seeing it as a rational challenge to religious faith. It may seem difficult to explain why God allows suffering and evil, but to many it may seem just as difficult to understand what any God, who wishes a worshipful response from humans, should make it so difficult to believe by providing so many competing faiths.

Philosophical issues about the nature of religion are intractable enough, and the relationship between faith and reason is an exceedingly venerable topic. The fact, though, of different religions also raises many political issues. How can people of different religious beliefs, and none, live together, without the conflict that seems only too evident in many parts of the contemporary world? The tensions produced by religious differences, even in democratic societies, produce challenges at every level of society. Courts in Western countries often find cases about the treatment of different religions, and various believers, among the most problematic and controversial that they have to deal with.

This book will deal with the underlying philosophical issues of how religion, and religious difference, is to be understood. I am also very aware that there is a more practical side to the issues, with major concerns about how to deal with religious differences in divided societies. Should religion be given any special treatment in society? How far should different kinds of religious conscience be accommodated? Is religious freedom of particular importance as a human right? What should children be taught about religion in state schools? All modern societies have to face these questions, and this book will not shirk them.

One constant temptation in facing major cultural differences is to take refuge in one form or another of relativism. Each group must live by their own truth, but there is no overarching "truth" that all should recognise. I have argued consistently for the incoherence of such a position since I first wrote about it, with reference both to religion and science, in my *Reason and Commitment* (1973). During the succeeding generation, relativism, as an explicit doctrine, became ever more widespread, not least through so-called "post-modernism." Such philosophical ideas can gradually have an effect on society as a whole, but they are at their most dangerous, when they merely take the form of conventional wisdom, and are not explicitly articulated, let alone rationally challenged. The same goes for an unthinking faith in science as the ultimate arbiter of everything. I continued to write in favour of a broad-based reason in, among other books, *Rationality and Science: Can Science Explain Everything?* (1993) and *Rationality and Religion: Does Faith Need Reason?* (1998).

Since then, religion has become an even more crucial issue both on the world stage, and within Western countries. Growing religious diversity, coupled with further moves to a more active secularism in the West, has been coupled with a marked growth in commitment to various religions, not least Christianity and Islam, in other countries across the globe. All this, it seems, can no longer be ignored either by law or politics. I have tried to deal with some of the issues arising in *Religion in Public Life: Must Faith be Privatized?* (2007) and *Equality, Freedom and Religion* (2012). Many of these problems are impossible to ignore in societies which have become religiously diverse. It is inevitable that the mere fact of religious diversity should come under philosophical scrutiny, and this is what I do in this book, whilst not forgetting the wider social, political and legal contexts. I also try to place contemporary disputes against their wider historical background.

The book was greatly aided by my work in Oxford with colleagues there. I have also been an Associate Scholar of the Religious Freedom Project, directed by Dr. Thomas F. Farr, at the Berkley Center for Religion, Peace and World Affairs in Georgetown University, Washington, DC, and funded by the John Templeton Foundation. I was stimulated by the many ideas I encountered at the various seminars and conferences organized in association with the Project. Not least, they gave an international context, which demonstrated how problems of religious diversity, and of religious freedom, have a global salience. I am particularly grateful to Tom Farr himself, to Dr. Timothy Shah, and to Kyle Van der Meulen for all the help and friendship they have given me.

As always, I owe more than I can say to my family, to my wife, Julia, to my daughter, Dr. Alison Teply, and my son-in law, Robert Teply, all of whom have helped me in significant ways to write this book.

Roger Trigg, St Cross College, Oxford

THE CHALLENGE OF RELIGIOUS DIVERSITY

THE PROBLEM OF DIVERSITY

The contemporary world echoes with such phrases as "celebrating diversity." As contact between even previously remote parts of the world increases, we cannot fail to be aware of the great diversity of belief and practice that exists around the world in all areas of human life. Modern technology can ensure that even tribes in New Guinea can see what is happening at that moment in New York. The increase of air travel between continents enables all of us to become tourists in every part of the globe, and many to move their homes and jobs to countries of which a few years ago they may not even have heard. There is migration from one European country to another, even though in living memory those countries may have been at war with each other, or at least totally isolated from each other's way of life. Barriers between Eastern and Western Europe set up after the Second World War have disappeared.

All this is commonplace, although it gives sociologists plenty of material on which to build theories about "globalization." None of us can live in hermetically sealed societies, assuming that our way of life is not only the best way but the only way. Differing ways of life compete for our attention even in the same place. In such a ferment of change, most people on the top of a London bus may be speaking any language but English. There used to be a saying about "the man on the Clapham omnibus" meaning, a hundred years or so ago, the average person in the street. One could use such a mythical London figure to illustrate "ordinary," "normal" reactions to whatever was under discussion. A short trip on any London bus today will quickly dispel any hope of distilling any common reaction to anything. Languages, cultures, and religions clash in merry profusion. All the people on the bus have in common is that they are in the same place at the same time. They are, of course, all human, and their share in a common human nature may not be a trivial issue. It may provide them all with a commonality on which all else is built. We will return to that. Nevertheless the immediate impact is the fact of difference and diversity.

At a trivial level, this makes life more interesting. We have a myriad of different ethnic foods and restaurants from which to choose. At a deeper level, however, it can appear very destabilizing for any society, which becomes afraid of a loss of identity. Beliefs can no longer be assumed to be shared. Social cohesion is put in jeopardy if we all disagree, perhaps violently, about what we think most important for our own lives and for society. Indeed, do we all even belong to the same society any longer? If neither religion nor language is shared, there may be few shared beliefs, assumptions, or customs to bind people together.

The need for a common identity may be one side of the coin, but another is the need to avoid conflict with those who disagree with us, either on an individual or group basis. In all this, religion has played a central role, both as an aggravating feature and as a source of reconciliation. Religion typically is concerned with what humans think is ultimately most important in life. It defines their ultimate commitments. Indeed, some, such as the twentieth-century Protestant theologian Paul Tillich, have linked religious faith explicitly with ideas of "ultimate concern" and the "the really ultimate."[1] He says, for instance: "The question of faith is not Moses or Jesus or Mohammed: the question is: Who expresses most adequately one's ultimate concern."[2] In this it looks as if religious faith is being defined in terms of whatever is thought of ultimate importance. Whatever governs my life is of ultimate concern to me, and hence is my religion. That probably would mean that everyone has a religion, even if it is focused on what in most people's eyes may be rather trivial.

There is a story of an English football manager, to whom it was said that football was clearly his religion. His quick retort was: "Oh no – it is much more important than that!" The joke depends on the fact

---

1 See Paul Tillich, *Dynamics of Faith*, Allen and Unwin, London, 1957, p. 96.
2 Tillich, *Dynamics of Faith*, p. 66.

that religion is not just a matter of passionate commitment and personal concern, but of a belief in some form of ultimate reality. Football can be a life's passion, but it is not concerned with the ultimate reality behind the universe, or with a life beyond this physical one. Religions typically are.

It is notoriously hard to define what "religion" means, not least because the temptation is to define it in terms familiar to us. Other religions, to be recognized as such, would have to be described in terms belonging to our own religion. Some definitions of religion could refer to "God" and make monotheism the defining feature of religion, but that must be too limiting. "Religion" is not just Christianity writ large, so that something only counts as religious if it coheres with what may be recognizable to Christian belief. That is too ethnocentric. Some views of religion see monotheism as itself a development, even a progression, from polytheistic forms of belief. Just as science needed the idea of one reality as an object of rational investigation, so true religion, the argument might go, needed to see that there could only be one Creator ultimately responsible for the whole Universe, and be the Creator of it. Even that view, however, tacitly assumes that monotheism (and probably Judeo-Christian monotheism at that) is the proper destination, and that religious development is a "value-laden" progress to something better.

Once we empty the idea of religion of what is most familiar, the concept itself may seem to gain little purchase. Yet the opposite danger – of defining religion too narrowly – can itself be pernicious. If a claim for religious freedom is laid before a court of law, it may, in some jurisdictions, matter whether a practice is "religious" or not. It is very easy for, say, an English court to assume that freedom of religion assumes a freely chosen commitment by an individual. It can then find it hard[3] to understand traditional definitions of being Jewish through matrilineal descent, and count this as a mere ethnic matter, without any issue of it being a theological matter for Jews. The idea of being born into a religion, rather than choosing it, may be strange to English Protestants, but it is a familiar notion in many religions, including Islam. Religion and ethnicity can merge, and indeed have done so in many societies in which religious diversity has not been fully acknowledged.

---

3 As in the case *R v. JFS*, (2009) UKSC 15, concerning criteria for admission to a Jewish school.

THE GROWTH OF FREEDOM

Despite the fact of an Established Church in England, there has never been any settled agreement about religion there since the Reformation. Roman Catholicism was always a latent force, practiced in some prominent families, lingering on in Elizabethan times, and implicated in the Gunpowder Plot to blow up the House of Parliament in 1605. On the other wing of the Church of England, Puritanism was soon causing separatist tendencies, with the first Baptist congregations taking root at the beginning of the seventeenth century and, as we shall see, producing demands for greater religious freedom. These tendencies, themselves producing splits between different brands of Protestantism, eventually exploded in the English Civil War of the seventeenth century. After that, and the Restoration both of King and Established Church, James II still tried to reintroduce Roman Catholicism into England, and had to flee on suspicion of attempting to establish an absolute monarchy.

Thus the accession of William and Mary in the Glorious Revolution,[4] and the Act of Toleration of 1689, provided a landmark in English history and the development of democracy. It recognized the pluralism that was endemic in English society, and no longer tied the idea of citizenship to adherence to one form of religion. The rights of "nonconformists" who stood apart from the Church of England were at last recognized, though it took many years for all distinctions between Anglicans and non-Anglicans to be eradicated. It was not until the nineteenth century, for instance, before entry to Oxford and Cambridge was broadened. Roman Catholics, too, remained under suspicion, and even John Locke, the great apostle of religious toleration and the Glorious Revolution's "official" philosopher, found it difficult not to remain suspicious of their allegiance to a foreign ruler (the Pope). Added to this, continuing Jacobite agitation in support of James II and his descendants remained a threat to the Protestant throne of England and Scotland until well on in the eighteenth century.

This pluralism, in the sociological sense of there being different forms of religious belief and expression within one society, was exported to the American Colonies. The strains this caused were particularly noticeable

---

4 See S. Pincus, *1688, The First Modern Revolution*, Yale University Press, New Haven, 2009.

in Virginia, where the Church of England was established, but as the eighteenth century progressed, other denominations such as Presbyterians and Baptists become both more numerous and more vociferous.[5] They resented Anglican privilege. Indeed, without a resident bishop, the Bishop of London provided Episcopal authority from far away. The result was that local gentry were not only prominent in the politics of the Colony but, through their "vestries" or church councils, were in charge of the maintenance of the Church and its ministry. Indeed the vestries were also a functioning local government, looking after the needs of the poor. As a result, non-Anglicans felt marginalized and resented paying taxes to support the Anglican clergy.

A society with a dominant church that was not supported by a considerable number of its citizens was clearly heading for trouble, particularly when coercive taxes were still being enforced. Virginia proved to be the cradle of demands for equal rights, and in particular for the right to freedom of religion. Even in the years leading up to 1776, there were regular prosecutions of dissenters, particularly Baptists, for such offenses as taking unauthorized services or unauthorized preaching, or even for failing to attend the Anglican parish church.[6] In protest against such a limitation on personal liberty, Virginians such as Thomas Jefferson, George Mason, and James Madison all played key roles in the establishment of freedom of religion as a basic American norm, as expressed in what became the First Amendment to the U.S. Constitution, saying that "Congress shall make no law respecting an establishment of religion or prohibiting the free exercise thereof."

The irony was that this was certainly a reaction to Anglican Establishment as practiced in Virginia, but Virginia had failed to keep pace with the expectation of "tolerance" for dissenters or nonconformists that had been required by the English Act of Toleration of 1689. The applicability of actions by the Westminster Parliament to the various colonies was a continuing bone of contention, but it is striking that, at least before the War of Independence, the British authorities were inclined

---

5 See John A. Ragosta *Wellspring of Liberty: How Virginia's Dissenters Helped Win the American Revolution and Secured Religious Liberty*, Oxford University Press, New York, 2010.
6 See Appendix A in Ragosta, *Wellsprings of Liberty*, pp. 171–183.

to champion a religious freedom that was becoming more familiar in England at the time.

The British Lords of Trade indeed responded to an inquiry by the acting Governor of Virginia by saying that "a free Exercise of Religion is so valuable a branch of true liberty, and so essential to the enriching and improving of a Trading Nation, it should ever be held sacred in His Majesty's Colonies."[7] In 1769, the new Governor said to Presbyterian clergy that "it is the King's express command that liberty of conscience be allowed to all his subjects, so they be contented with a quiet and peaceable enjoyment of the same." Presbyterians would very likely be resentful of Anglican privilege, as many would be immigrants from Scotland who would feel that their own established church, the Presbyterian Church of Scotland, deserved as much recognition as the established Church of England. The feeling that privileges for one group inevitably make those who are not members of that group feel devalued and less than full citizens is an issue that echoes through all debates about the role of religion in a society in which there are differing beliefs. It offends against demands for equality.[8]

What is remarkable is that the British authorities were using phrases such as the "free exercise of religion" and "liberty of conscience" in contrast to the efforts of the Virginian gentry to impose an ecclesiastical uniformity. Yet it would only be few years before those same phrases would be used against the British. The argument that it was "good for trade" was partly that it would encourage settlers of different backgrounds. Of deeper interest, however, is the argument from principle, particularly the implication that as "a branch of true liberty," religious liberty is deeply linked with all other democratic freedoms. That was certainly a view held by the American Founders. They were confronted, as in England, with differing religious denominations, with different ways of organizing themselves. Freedom of religion typically meant freedom for different varieties of Christianity to flourish, even if there was an initial reluctance to extend that to Roman Catholicism.

Once the principle of religious liberty is accepted, however, it has to be extended to all varieties of religious conscience, protecting even

7 Ragosta, *Wellsprings of Liberty*, p. 41.
8 See Roger Trigg, *Equality, Freedom and Religion*, Oxford University Press, Oxford, 2012.

those who wish to repudiate all religion. The difficulty of giving a tight definition of religion then becomes salient. It is tempting to say that beliefs in the supernatural and in a life beyond the physical one are the most typical signs of a religious belief, although this might rule out pantheism, the idea that God or gods are identical with the natural world. Links with a way of life, incorporating typical moral behavior, may also seem central to a religion, but some religions, such as ancient Greek and Roman polytheism, concentrated on public ritual. Their gods were hardly exemplars of morality. The communal aspect of religion may seem important, so that religion might be defined as a particular form of social practice, but again, religions may differ radically on how much stress is to be placed on individual belief and commitment rather than public practice.

The twentieth-century philosopher Ludwig Wittgenstein has tried to define games by looking for a common feature, but in the end said they had a "family resemblance." There is no single feature that all games have in common. They are not all played with balls, for instance, although many are. Nor do all of them have game pieces, like chess and cards, for example. As Wittgenstein says of games, "if you look at them you will not see something that is common to *all*, but similarities, relationships, and a whole series of them at that."[9] Wittgenstein wanted us to get away from the assumption that if we have a word, there must be one thing that it names. He wanted us to look at how words are used. Indeed he said that we must "bring words back from their metaphysical to their everyday use." The later Wittgenstein had changed his mind about how language functioned, and reacted against his early work. He argued against the propensity of philosophers to use a word such as "object" or "being" or even "name" and to try to grasp the "essence" of the thing. He asked, "Is the word ever actually used in this way in the language-game which is its original home?"[10]

This is the edge of a major philosophical argument about how language functions and whether its prime purpose is to pick out and identify an objective reality. It is, as we shall see, a crucial issue for religious belief. Wittgenstein, in his later work, was concerned to see how language was actually used, and its connection with our wider practices. He

9 Ludwig Wittgenstein, *Philosophical Investigations* #66, Basil Blackwell, Oxford, 1958.
10 Wittgenstein, *Philosophical Investigations*, #116.

would ask what difference the use of word makes to our life. Following Wittgenstein, much modern philosophy has reacted against "essentialism," looking for the one feature that makes something what it is. The pursuit of a clear definition of religion may be a hopeless task, and courts in many jurisdictions, when faced with allegations of religious discrimination and such like, typically shrink from it. They realize that any definition on which they alight may arbitrarily exclude a practice, or involve them in unwanted discussions of theology. A series of similarities and relationships connecting different "religions" may be enough. Just as it may be difficult even to decide borderlines cases of what is red rather than, say, orange, but we know that red is not green, similarly drawing a sharp line between religious and nonreligious manifestations may be difficult, but we know that football is not a candidate for a religion.

DEMOCRATIC DIVERSITY

Is religious diversity a good thing? If freedom of religion is closely linked to our other freedoms, diversity of belief would seem to be the inevitable result. The difficulty of pinning down a common feature in all religion shows how, in looking for similarity, we are confronted by diversity. It goes far beyond the mere splintering of Protestant Christianity into different denominations. Diversity stretches far beyond differences within one religion and comprehends all religions and none. One cannot assume that there is a bedrock of general Christian belief uniting virtually all citizens, as was the case in seventeenth-century England or eighteenth-century Virginia.

Even so, disagreement and conflict on religious issues brought into sharp focus the need for tolerance and the link between diversity and freedom. If people are to live freely in a democratic society, in which all citizens can contribute to discussions about the common good, they must be free to make up their own minds on where the common good may lie. This will bring into play their most basic beliefs about human nature and the place of humans in the world. Their religious outlook, or lack of one, is bound to be relevant. If I am expected to conform to an external orthodoxy and not dare even to raise questions about its basis, the whole notion of free democratic debate and decision making has to be jettisoned. This is true whether the orthodoxy is religious or antireligious in character.

Pluralism, in the sense of the existence of different beliefs, whether religious or not, would appear to be the very stuff of democracy. The latter is a mechanism for settling disputes. If we all naturally agreed about everything, there would be no need for all the machinery of democracy, debate, elections, decision making by majority vote, and the rest. Democracy is a method of coping with diversity of opinion. The existence of different beliefs and views is a precondition for good decision making. Choices are not choices if alternatives cannot be presented. If the same opinions are imposed on everyone through coercion, we may all go wrong in a big way. We are not omniscient, and there can be no guarantee that any views are the right ones. Some religious positions, and some secular totalitarian regimes, have claimed to know what is true, with the concomitant right of imposing "right beliefs" on everyone, but democratic states are structured on the assumption that some people do not know better than others do. Plato in the *Republic* hankered after rulers who would possess knowledge, and it was no accident that he was extremely skeptical of the virtues of democracy after seeing how a mob could be swayed in ancient Athens.

In the contemporary world, democracy is not universally admired, partly because of the diversity of belief it implies. Some Muslims, particularly those of a more "fundamentalist" persuasion, are particularly wary of it because it appears to put humans, and not God, in control of events. They may look at the increasing secularization of many Western societies and link that to the way in which representative government seems to deal more with the satisfaction of the various preferences of citizens, and their pressing material concerns, rather than any perceived obligation to God. Democracy is seen of its nature not just to provide a mechanism for managing disagreement and diversity, but also as a means of promoting both. It stresses the role of competing views while allegedly ignoring issues of religious truth. All this, of course, raises the pressing question of who knows what God's will is and where any particular truth lies. Clearly, like Plato's philosopher-kings, some have to claim to be in special possession of truth if they do not wish to allow democratic debate and decision making.

It is undeniable that diversity and democracy go together. Diversity of belief provides the context that makes democratic ways of settling disputes desirable. It is also the product of democracy, since democratic freedom enables many different systems of belief to be put forward and perhaps flourish. This is important in politics, and also in religion. The enforcement of any one religious outlook must be the death of all democracy because it strikes at its roots. If people are not free to make up their own minds about what is important in life, there can be no proper democratic debate. We have seen that religion is characteristically concerned with what humans think most important in life. The idea of a God or gods, and the possibility of a life beyond this, brings with it the idea that this world itself might be imbued with purpose, having been specially created. It then matters what each one of us does, and there are objective standards of right and wrong, good and bad, which may be built into the very nature of things, and are independent of human decision.

The assertion, or denial, of such beliefs goes to the heart of people's ideas of what is important in life and what should be valued. The idea that humans themselves have a special importance, and that therefore human rights should be respected, certainly has religious roots. Yet the very stress on individual judgment that goes with democracy can pose hard questions about the role of religion. Once the idea of an infallible authority, even if benign, is removed, each individual may appear free to make up his or her own mind. All, it may be said, are entitled to their own opinions. "That is just your opinion" is a favorite retort in an argument. One writer suggests that this kind of extreme individualism means that "the supreme value is individual choice per se, regardless of what is chosen."[11]

Yet does that mean that all opinions are equally valid? People may hesitate to say that this is so in some areas such as science. It is difficult to see the point of science if it is not in the business of searching for truth and ultimate agreement. The whole idea of scientific progress depends on the hope that we are slowly gaining more knowledge about the physical world. Philosophers of science have often claimed that a diversity of scientific theory is an indispensable means of arriving at the truth. If one idea does not work, we have to be able to turn to another. A science warped by ideology, demanding answers in one direction only, is on a sure path to disaster. Biology in the Soviet Union became corrupted by communist ideology in this way. Freedom is a necessary

---

11 Brad S. Gregory, *The Unintended Reformation*, Belknap Press of Harvard University Press, Cambridge, MA, 2012, p. 176.

component of the search for truth in science, and it will be in every human endeavor.

James Madison, in eighteenth-century Virginia, did not doubt the centrality of religious freedom in the general search for freedom, and he saw religious diversity as itself a guarantee of that freedom. As one of the authors of the U.S. Constitution and of the subsequent Bill of Rights, and eventually as President of the United States, he was very involved in original arguments over the ratification of the Constitution by the thirteen original states. For him, the whole idea of checks and balances sprang from the existence of different interest groups, so that power could never be concentrated in one group, let alone a single individual. In explaining and defending the proposed Constitution, he wrote in the *Federalist Papers* about the importance of deriving authority from society, or "the people," but broken up into many interest groups and classes of citizens. In other words, democracy itself depended on the existence of differing beliefs and understandings, so that one view could never dominate. It assumed, and needed, the existence of a variegated, pluralist society. He continued in a very significant manner by saying: "In a free government the security for civil rights must be the same as that for religious rights. It consists in the one case in the multiplicity of interests, and in the other in the multiplicity of sects. The degree of security in both cases will depend on the number of interests and sects."[12]

In other words, a religious pluralism, in which many sects and denominations flourish, was to be welcomed, so that one denomination could not dominate the others and challenge their rights. Whenever, Madison thought, a majority is united by a common interest, whether religious or secular, "the rights of the minority will be insecure."[13]

To what extent, however, should the interests of minorities be recognized? We have already indicated that the future of democracy depends on the production and maintenance of alternative views. Reasoned opposition to the government should not be restrained, because it is the nature of democracy to allow such opposition the chance to go even as far as to form an alternative government. Democracy needs a continual ferment of ideas. Yet, although the existence of religious sects and

---

12 James Madison, "Federalist Papers 51," in *The Federalist Papers*, ed. Clinton Rossiter, Signet Classic, New York, 2003, p. 321.
13 Madison, *Federalist Papers*, p. 320.

denominations may be regarded in the same way from the standpoint of civil society, things may not be so simple given the theological outlook of the various groups.

Madison was particularly concerned, given his background in Virginia, about the problems arising when a dominant religious view attempts to coerce minorities, as Anglicans had been doing there with Baptists and Presbyterians. He even objected to the attempt in Virginia to give financial support to all the Christian denominations, saying in his famous "Memorial and Remonstrance against Religious Assessments"[14] that any government support of religion, however widely spread, "degrades from the equal rank of citizens all those whose opinions in religion do not bend to those of the legislative authority."[15] Moreover, he believed, such an assertion of governmental authority in the religious sphere may be distant from the Inquisition, "but it differs from it only in degree."[16] It represents the first step in a downward spiral of intolerance. At the time Madison wrote this, the Inquisition had still not been finally abolished in parts of Catholic Europe, and was to survive officially in Spain until 1834. It was still, in the eighteenth century, a terrifying warning of the out-workings of religious intolerance.

Yet the Inquisition in its various forms within Europe (and in Latin America) had existed to promote what was regarded as truth. The idea of a truth that is thought to hold for everyone but which is not recognized by everyone can be immensely troubling. Should all be made to see it? This is not just an issue for any religion that claims truth. The holders of any ideology, such as communism, can also hold that they are in a privileged position to understand what is true, and that they are somehow entitled to impose it on others for their own good.

IS RELIGION ONLY SUBJECTIVE?

Religions seem to impart a certainty about truth that drives practitioners to want to coerce others. This has been a permanent shadow cast by

---

14 James Madison, "Memorial and Remonstrance," in *The Separation of Church and State*, ed. Forrest Church, Beacon Press, Boston, 2004, p. 67.
15 For a discussion of the importance of equality in such contexts, see Trigg, *Equality, Freedom and Religion*.
16 Madison, "Memorial and Remonstrance," p. 67.

many forms of religion through the centuries. One way of preventing such an approach is to deny that religion can claim such knowledge in the first place. Indeed, it may be alleged, all religion must come under epistemological suspicion. It is not the kind of thing that can be publicly established according to commonly accepted criteria of reason. As such, it may be fit for private devotion but should not be paraded in the public square.[17] A constant theme, as we shall see, is that the very diversity of religious belief, particularly in comparison with science, gives weight to suspicions about the status of alleged religious "knowledge." The argument is summed up as follows: "The multiplicity and radically diverse content of religious truth claims, it is argued, point to religion's arbitrary, subjective character, so dramatically different from the cross-cultural universality of highly corroborated, modern scientific theories such as the theory of evolution."[18]

Just how pervasive this view is can be measured by the fact that it has influenced the administration of English law. In a judgment subsequently quoted with approval by judges in other cases, Lord Justice Laws in the Court of Appeal for England and Wales resisted any idea that the law should protect any position on the ground that it was upheld by particular religion, in this case Christianity.[19] It was his reason for holding this that was troubling, however. He said that this would be to impose compulsory law (i.e., to coerce) "not to advance the general good on objective grounds, but to give effect to the force of subjective opinion." He continued:

This must be so, since in the eye of everyone save the believer religious faith is necessarily subjective, being incommunicable by any kind of proof or evidence. It may of course be true; but the ascertainment of such a truth lies beyond the means by which laws are made in a reasonable society. Therefore it lies only in the heart of the believer, who is alone bound by it. No-one else is or can be so bound, unless by his own free choice he accepts its claims.[20]

Lord Justice Laws further condemns the irrationality in promulgating law concerning a position held purely on religious grounds given that

---

17 See Roger Trigg, *Religion in Public Life: Must Religion be Privatized?* Oxford University Press, Oxford, 2007.

18 Gregory, *The Unintended Reformation*, p. 76.

19 Also discussed more fully in Trigg, *Equality, Freedom and Religion*, pp. 142–145.

20 *McFarlane v Relate Ltd* (2010) EWCA Civ B1 Para 23.

it prefers "the subjective over the objective."[21] This all neatly sums up a modern prejudice that all religious faith is subjective and cannot be justified on objective grounds, let alone be subjected to any ordinary standard of proof or evidence. It is as subjective as my dislike of bananas, which may be true about me but says nothing about how you do or should react. Tastes are personal, and not all share the same ones. The same, it seems, is true of religion. This approach has the virtue that we can simultaneously respect people's individual religious beliefs, in the sense that we do not stop them from having them, and also make it clear that they can have no relevance to other people's decisions, let alone to how they should conduct their lives.

The issue of what is subjective and what is objective needs careful definition. Saying that religion makes no objective claims must mean that it cannot concern an objective reality, accessible to all. Even stressing that only a scientific means of observation and experiment provide an objective methodology entails that we talk only of a reality accessible to science. Any stress on subjectivity is an attack on the idea that subjective beliefs can claim truth. They are not about anything, but merely exhibit a stance that is valid only for the person expressing it. Something that claims truth must in principle be open to rational examination by everyone. If it is only subjectively valid, it is not concerned with truth that holds for the rest of us. It merely tells us about the person.

The demands of religious freedom may mean that we ought to respect diverse religious views we may not share. That is different from the question of truth. The fact that someone holds a belief is one thing. What the belief is about and whether it can be rationally defended is another. Lord Justice Laws intervened in a centuries-old debate about the respective roles of faith and reason. In any discussion of the fact of religious diversity, the question of the status of faith in a religious context cannot be ignored. If the judge is right, reason and faith are opposed to each other. Religion can take no part in a reasonable discussion. It cannot pass any judgement worth taking notice of on what constitutes the general good. Faith is subjective and personal, and cannot have any public dimension, let alone make any claim to objectivity.

21 *McFarlane*, Para 24.

There are good political reasons for this stance, in that it enables a respect for people's individual religious stances to be maintained while ensuring that their beliefs can gain no purchase in public life, let alone influence law. It is to suggest that faith is a magic ingredient that some people may have and others do not, but that it is mysteriously totally unrelated to the world around, so that it is not susceptible to reasoned argument, and certainly cannot contribute in any rational manner to public debate. Yet that is to ignore the simple fact that all faith has to be faith in something or somebody. There is no such thing as undirected faith.

RELIGION AND TRUTH

When anyone claims to have faith, or someone else talks of a person's faith, it is relevant what that faith is in, or in other words, what kind of faith it is. This applies even in nonreligious cases. If I claim to have faith in my doctor, perhaps having faith that he can cure me, it does matter that my beliefs about the doctor are justified. If he was run over by a bus this morning, my faith can no longer hold even if I do not realize that. If the doctor's marvellous qualifications that have so impressed me are in fact fake, again my faith is unjustified and I am deluded. I may still trust him, but my trust is totally unwarranted. So it must be with religious faith. I have to be able to specify in what God or gods I have faith. I must have beliefs about them, which might justify my trust. Those beliefs can be challenged, and above all it may just be false that such a deity, or deities, exist in the first place.

It may be retorted that this is begging the question that assertions about God are open to rational examination. What make them subjective is precisely the lack of possible evidence for or against and the inability of reason to get a grip on the issue. Lord Justice Laws talked of an ordinary standard of proof or evidence Yet it is not hard to see here the long shadow of an outmoded empiricism. Before and after World War II, the so-called Vienna Circle had an immense influence in encouraging the view that all philosophy must be science based, and that what was needed was a scientific conception of the world. The movement influenced not only the philosophy of science but all philosophy and was known as logical positivism. It was popularized in Britain by the philosopher A.J. Ayer in his influential book, *Language,*

Truth and Logic.[22] Its particular target was metaphysics, and enormous stress was placed on the need for empirical verification of everything claimed. If we do not know how to check an assertion by scientific means, seeing what could count for or against through observation or experiment, then it is literally a meaningless statement.

The claim that religious statements are of only subjective validity is not far from this, because it is being maintained that believers are not making substantive assertions about reality. According to those who do not believe that religious beliefs should be imported into public debate, they are not making claims about an objective reality that can be of relevance to others. They are not saying anything beyond evincing an attitude to the world. In a parallel move over moral statements, Ayer claimed that they could not assert anything either, but were merely expressing emotion. To say that stealing is wrong is just like saying "boo" to stealing. The assertion merely tells us about the speaker's attitudes.

If I say there is a heffalump in the garden, but cannot specify what a heffalump is, or how one would detect one, it is beginning to look not only that I do not know what I talking about, but that I am quite possibly not talking about anything. Is talk of a God like that, because it cannot be checked by ordinary scientific means? The claim that all metaphysical claims, including religious ones, were literally meaningless, a mere string of sounds, challenged many. It is easier to argue with those who claim that what you say is false than with those who claim to find it unintelligible nonsense.

Some scientists such as Richard Dawkins have espoused a "scientistic" view of the world, giving absolute epistemological priority to science and to what can be discovered through scientific method. Dawkins can thus say that "God's existence or non-existence is a scientific fact about the universe, discoverable in principle like any other."[23] Arguments, therefore, from natural theology arguing from the nature of the physical world to God could be relevant, but Dawkins considers the existence of God highly improbable on scientific grounds. This is not as devastating an argument as those of the logical positivists about the meaningfulness of religious language, although Dawkins, like Ayer, ties

22 A. J. Ayer, *Language Truth and Logic*, 2nd ed., Victor Gollancz, London, 1946.
23 Richard Dawkins, *The God Delusion*, Bantam Press, London, 2006, p. 54.

rationality to scientific method, and assumes that "evidence" can only be scientific evidence. At least, however, there seems to be the possibility of some rational discussion, with atheists denying what theists wanted to assert.

In the case of verificationism, which tied both meaning and truth to human experience and to science, atheism was strictly an impossibility, as one cannot deny a claim that cannot even be properly formed. Religious belief of all kinds, it seemed, could not be making claims about an objective reality. What then were religious people doing with the language they were using? If it had any function, it could not be that of claiming truth. In the 1950s in particular, philosophers of religion grappled with this issue as they tried to salvage something in the face of the hostility of much contemporary philosophy.

Why does this matter for the issue of religious diversity? A fundamental fact about different religions is that they often appear to contradict each other. Buddhists may find it difficult to accept the idea of a God who created everything. Muslims, Jews, and Christians differ about the importance of the person of Christ, and over such doctrines as the Christian view of a Trinitarian God. One could go on. Religious understandings vary. The stories told in different religions vary. A normal understanding would be that they are all contradicting each other, and fighting, sometimes literally, about what is true. Therefore, each of them would conclude that religious diversity is a major problem. Why cannot everyone agree when confronted with truth? The subversive thought must be that truth is not in play here.

The verificationist challenge is relevant to this problem. If the idea of truth in religion is an illusion, either all religions can be dismissed entirely, or they should not be understood as being in the truth claiming business. They may not be the threat to each other they so often seem. One extreme reaction to positivism came in an influential article from 1955 by the Cambridge philosopher R. B. Braithwaite.[24] His explanation of religion and religious statements was that "the primary use of religious assertions is to announce allegiance to a set of moral principles." Religion is more than that expression of intention, however,

---

24 R. B. Braithwaite, "An Empiricist's View of the Nature of Religious Belief," in *The Philosophy of Religion*, ed. Basil Mitchell, Oxford University Press, Oxford, 1971, pp. 72–91.

according to Braithwaite. He thinks that religions may recommend the same way of life but are "associated with thinking of different stories." He explains by saying:

On the assumption that the ways of life advocated by Christians and Buddhists are essentially the same, it will be the fact that the intention to follow this way of life is associated in the mind of the Christian with thinking of one set of stories (the Christian ones), while it is associated in the mind of the Buddhist with thinking of another set of stories (the Buddhist stories) which enables a Christian assertion to be distinguished from a Buddhist one.[25]

Braithwaite is at pains to point out that to tell the story is not necessarily to make an empirical claim. The story does not have to be believed to be true. It can just be inspiring, with a psychological effect. In this way he could retain a function for religious language while not falling afoul of a tough-minded empiricist philosopher, who wanted no truck with the transcendent or metaphysical. Yet he implies that believers do not properly understand the way they were using language, and are mistaken if they thought they were claiming truth.

It did not escape the notice of some philosophers that there was a positive gain in removing some of controversial claims that religions made in opposition to each other. If the main doctrines of different religions could be given the status of stories or myths (a favorite word), perhaps they are not really in conflict. They are just entertaining different narratives while going in the same direction. Differences could be minimized at the philosophical level, and this could give rise to greater mutual respect and understanding. The pursuit of truth, it appeared, could be harmful. Far better, it might seem, to show that truth was not at stake. There are just different ways of life.

Typical of this approach was a book that attained some notoriety in the 1970s, called *The Myth of God Incarnate*. In a sense, the title says it all. A group of philosophers and theologians attempted to show that the doctrine of the Incarnation, of God becoming man in the person Christ, was a myth, itself a term of art, but intended to imply that whatever profundities the doctrine expressed, it was not literally true. The connection between the urge to revise the doctrine and a willingness to be open to other religions was articulated by the influential philosopher

25 Braithwaite, p. 84.

of religion, John Hick, who was the editor of the volume. In an article in the book entitled "Jesus and the World Religions," he wrote: "If Jesus was literally God incarnate, and if it is by his death alone that men can be saved, and by their response to him alone that they can appropriate that salvation, then the only doorway to eternal life is Christian faith. It would follow from this that the large majority of the human race so far have not been saved."[26]

This runs together issues of truth and salvation, which are distinct. It may be true that there is a God revealed uniquely in Christ. What that entails for those who have never even heard the name of Jesus is another matter, and brings in issues about the alleged mercy of God. Even if, however, we concentrate for the moment on the issue of truth, what is the position of other religions when one religion claims to be true? Hick writes: "It seems clear that we are being called today to attain a global religious vision which is aware of the unity of all mankind before God and which at the same time makes sense of the diversity of God's ways within the various streams of human life."[27]

Hick was much influenced by his experience of growing religious diversity in Birmingham where he lived, following substantial immigration into England from Commonwealth countries. He wanted to further cooperation between the different religions. The issue, however, is whether a revision of religious doctrines to minimize differences is the right way to achieve that. At the time this meshed in with philosophical preoccupations with language. The pressing question arose as to whether the main function of religious language was to assert truth.

26 John Hick, ed., The *Myth of God Incarnate*, SCM Press, London, 1977, p. 180.
27 Hick, *The Myth of God Incarnate*, p.180.

2

DO RELIGIONS CLAIM TRUTH?

PLURALISM AND RELATIVISM

Religions that only express the personal attitudes of the believer cannot claim any truth that can be rationally assessed. Faith then is merely an idiosyncrasy that some have and some do not. As we have seen, however, this approach leaves unexplored the important issue of what faith is directed at. Is it the world, or reality? This question raises issues about truth, and if that becomes the monopoly of empirical science, religion is again pushed aside.

The fact that we can talk of different religions suggests that the notion of religious faith as a totally individual matter is misplaced. Faith is typically a body of belief and practice that is shared. The nature of truth is that it has to be communicated and learned. If truth is totally subjective, this means there can be no constraint on what I believe. I do not have to communicate my beliefs to others or learn from others, and my beliefs do not have to be measured in some way against the hard facts of reality. I can believe whatever I like, but that means that belief is pointless. The very idea of belief is intimately connected with holding something true, and if I realize it is only true for me, there might seem little point in believing that or anything else.

At the very least, if truth has any function, it has to be intersubjective. Others must be able to share it. I alone may feel my pain, but I must hope that others, particularly my doctor, will recognize my predicament as a real one. A total subjectivism brings the threat of nihilism. We lose grip on the idea that we live in the same world as others. Yet, a more seductive path can appear to await those who look at the different religions of the world and are reluctant to enter into judgment on them.

Subjectivism may seem incoherent, but a more subtle relativism can beckon. Relativism can have many forms, but one way of defining it is that what is true for a society, community, or other group is what they believe collectively. Truth is again wrenched from any connection with an objective reality confronted by all religions. It is instead constructed, and not discovered, as a collective enterprise. I may get out of step with my own community, and be judged wrong by their standards. There can, however, be no such thing as the whole community, or a whole religion, being mistaken. The Incarnation is true for Christians, and it is false for Moslems.

The word "pluralism" is much bandied around, and can be very slippery. From one point of view, it refers to the undoubted social fact that there are many religions and much religious disagreement. It is a sociological term, referring to something we all experience in contemporary life. From another point of view, the word can carry the assumption that there is no way in principle of standing outside of all religions and deciding which is true. Even from within a religion there cannot be any proper claim to a truth that applies to others even though they reject it. The claims about the nature of a transcendent reality, even of God, are relative to particular religions and can only claim validity from within them. There is nothing even to invoke in principle an alleged justification of the objective truth of any religion. That is relativism, in the sense being expounded here.

Even if pluralism does not slip into this relativism, it can carry with it the idea that religious diversity is positively good. The sociologist, Peter Berger, has distinguished between what he terms "plurality", which refers to the "social reality" of many religions, and pluralism. He claims that pluralism "is the attitude, possibly expanded into a full-blown philosophy, that *welcomes* the reality."[1] Welcoming the fact of many religions must itself be a significant step away from seeing them all as attempting to aim at the same truth. Given human finitude, it could be that varying insights into a transcendent reality are more likely to produce glimmerings of truth. Given religious disagreement, however, all of the different conceptions cannot be equally true if they contradict

---

1 Peter Berger and Anton Zijderveld, *In Praise of Doubt*, HarperOne, New York, 2009, p. 7.

each other. Jesus cannot both be the Son of God according to Christians and not be one according to Muslims. If all religions cannot be true, then perhaps none of them are.

Relativism may seem an easy refuge when we are faced with this problem. Religions are not, we might say, objectively true but are true according to their own lights and in the eyes of their own believers. Relativism might encourage mutual toleration of different religions. No religion can claim priority, but we can respect the sincerity and commitment of the different practitioners. Saying, however, that there is much truth in many religions is not consistent with relativism, because the idea that truth can even partially hold across religions is precisely what is being denied by this approach. Religions and communities in general are self-contained, with their own epistemological standards. Beliefs could overlap, but that idea does not hold in terms of truth.

One definition of relativism sees it not as the denial of objective truth, but that of any right to be certain of the truth one is claiming. Peter Berger and his coauthor Anton Zijderveld claim[2] that the opposite of relative is absolute. That may hold in some contexts, but it is confusing to use relativism in epistemological contexts to refer to a refusal to claim certainty rather than truth. Our knowledge, even in science, may sometimes be partial and uncertain, but that does not mean it is not knowledge. The physical sciences themselves progress on the assumption that knowledge about the physical universe can grow. Uncertainty, and doubt, does not entail that there is nothing to discover. Given a reality not of our own making, our understanding of it may be limited. That does not mean there is no reality, and our uncertainty in all branches of knowledge should be a spur to further effort.

The association of the idea of certainty with that of objective truth can encourage the adoption of relativism in the pursuit of an ideal of toleration. The idea of truth has often encouraged some to be certain that they possess it and that they have a right to impose it on others, perhaps in the interests of the victims. Some conclude that the only antidote is to remove what they see as the illusion of an objective truth that can inspire such arrogance. This line of thinking can be seen in the

---

2 Berger and Zijderveld, *In Praise of Doubt*, p. 25.

writings of the Italian postmodernist philosopher Gianni Vattimo. He opposes the idea of truth not only in religion but as a guiding concept in any context. He says, "[T]ruth is not encountered but constructed with consensus and respect for the liberty of everyone, and the diverse communities that live together, without blending, in a free society."[3] Truth is thus the product of agreement and not the correspondence of our beliefs and language with the way the world is. Vattimo appears to think that this will result in an increase in toleration, a reduction in authoritarianism, and the flourishing of democracy. This betrays an attitude that confuses certainty and dogmatism with the search for an objective truth that holds universally.

For Vattimo, truth "is the enemy of the open society and specifically of any democratic politics."[4] He says that "whenever truth becomes a factor in politics, the danger of authoritarianism rears its head."[5] His attack on truth is both general and specific, as he criticizes any belief in a God who "grounds" the human world, saying that it "clashes fatally with a culture that largely rejects the very notion of foundation or ground."[6] He has a particular criticism of the Roman Catholic Church's claim to speak on behalf of God.[7] He makes the biting comment that "when the Church feels weak it talks about freedom, and when it feels strong it talks about truth."[8]

Authoritarianism and a particular brand of certainty can go together, but it does not follow that if there is such a thing as objective truth (or the way the world is independent of our thought and language), we are automatically certain of what it is, or have any right to be so. The steps from reality and truth to our knowledge, to our certainty, and then to our willingness to coerce others are large. At each stage there is a gap, and crossing it needs justification. The fact that our knowledge does not construct reality but has to reflect it means that our understandings of the nature of reality may not be correct. Similarly, agreement may bring

3 Gianni Vattimo, *A Farewell to Truth*, Columbia University Press, New York, 2011, p. 36.
4 Vattimo, *A Farewell to Truth*, p. 2.
5 Vattimo, *A Farewell to Truth*, p. 12.
6 Vattimo, *A Farewell to Truth*, p. 50.
7 Vattimo, *A Farewell to Truth*, p. 50.
8 Vattimo, *A Farewell to Truth*, p. 53.

certainty, but that does not necessarily mean we are right. We have the confidence of mutual reassurance, but the world has always been full of people who have been certain and wrong. The reflection that this is the case can produce a philosophical skepticism that we can never know what is true. That is going too far, and we could never survive if we did not have many true beliefs about our environment.

REALISM AND ANTIREALISM

The belief in any reality, independent of individual and collective beliefs, can only encourage authoritarianism if we are sure we possess the whole truth. However, once we establish that reality is independent of all our knowledge and not a construction out of human knowledge, the logical gap between the two ensures that a claim of certainty cannot guarantee knowledge. Plato solved the problem through his doctrine of recollection (*anamnesis*). His "philosopher-kings" were supposedly able to cross the gap by recovering their innate knowledge of truth through a process of education. Certainly, once ontology (the theory of what there is) is detached from epistemology (our theory of how we can obtain knowledge), a pressing concern must always be on how to bridge that gap and to avoid total skepticism.

The existence of this gap ought to encourage an appropriate humility. We do not know, and cannot claim to know, everything about what there is. We should be prepared to listen, in science and elsewhere, to those with different conceptions, as we may be able to learn from them. Our knowledge is limited, as we humans are limited, not least by our position in time and space. This is definitely so in science. The other side of the universe, an interior of a black hole, or the nature of basic particles are all examples of physical reality that we grasp through theory, but which are beyond human observation. We may know more as science develops, but some of the physical world will always outstrip our ability to observe it or experience it in any way. Understanding that there is always more to discover drives science and forms the motivation and justification for scientific progress. If reality is merely a construction of our present ideas and agreements about it, then why not be content with what we have instead of restlessly looking to revise our views?

The assertion of the independence and "self-subsistence" of any form of reality, in whatever context, is called "realism," sometimes even "metaphysical realism."[9] Its opponents espouse various forms of "antirealism," but a common feature is that they talk of reality logically dependent on human understanding. They are typically anthropocentric. Even the logical positivists, with their stress on our intersubjective experience of a common world, make scientific reality dependent on what can be verified and falsified scientifically. That dependence links the nature of the world logically with what humans find accessible. It turns physical reality into empirical reality, namely what can be humanly experienced. The fact that before humans circled the moon, the existence of the other side of the moon raised problems for tough-minded empiricists says it all. What right have we to talk of what has not been experienced? An answer is to talk of what can in principle be experienced. As human technology evolves, more will come within our grasp. This, however, must be a surreptitious importation of realism, because it is tacitly understood that whatever exists is in principle open to be experienced.

The temptation to link logically whatever exists with human understanding is all pervasive. Relativists are quite content to see things in this antirealist manner, assuming that realities are in effect the shadow cast by people's collective beliefs. Perhaps, some may think, relativism carries the added bonus, compared with some forms of antirealism, that conceptions of reality are not based on what is in reach for humanity as a whole. The very profound differences that can exist between people are being taken into account. Relativists concentrate on divergences between communities, cultures, and conceptual systems. As well as tying reality to belief, they acknowledge the tremendous variation of belief that exists and are willing to talk of different realities and different worlds.

Many religions, however, see such relativism as corrosive of their beliefs. Once those who believe that something is true realize it is only true for "themselves," however they are collectively defined, a major motive for believing it must be removed. The relativism based on

9 For more on this, see Roger Trigg, *Reality at Risk: A Defence of Realism in Philosophy and the Sciences*, Harvester Wheatsheaf (Simon and Schuster), 2nd ed., Hemel Hempstead, 1989.

communities is as much a threat to religion as the subjectivism centered on individual belief. However, there is always a deep incoherence in any statement of relativism. The very assertion of relativism as a philosophical thesis in execution contradicts itself.[10] By speaking the words, I contradict what the words say. By claiming its validity I am, by asserting it, claiming a truth for everyone that the statement itself has to deny. It suggests that somehow I can stand outside all systems of belief and see that none of them can claim truth. If the implication is that none of them should be judged adversely by nonparticipants, the claim is probably that all religions are on a par with each other. As Italian philosopher Marcello Pera says: "The view that any given culture is equal in value to any other is no less doubtful than the view that a given culture is better than others. . . . The expression 'equal to' requires a common point of reference, which relativism does not allow us."[11]

Relativism may dismiss the notion of objective truth, but that dismissal itself assumes its own objective truth by ruling out alternatives. According to relativism, we have to be trapped within our societies and our own conceptual systems. The ideas of "conceptual relativism," that declare that different conceptual systems construct the world differently strike at the roots of any idea of a common rationality.[12] Different concepts then create different worlds and remove the possibility of any common basis. Conceptual divergence thus even removes any logical possibility of disagreement. One can no longer deny what another is asserting. Each talks past the other. There can be no common standard of what could count as true.

Parceling up our ideas into separate compartments cuts off different communities from each other. A dialogue between cultures and religions could never get started as we would have nothing in common once it has been denied that we all live in the same world and share the same human nature.[13] A consistent relativist cannot appeal to the commonality that

10 See, for instance Roger Trigg, *Reason and Commitment*, Cambridge University Press, Cambridge, 1973, chapter 1.
11 Marcello Pera *Why We Should Call Ourselves Christians: The Religious Roots of Free Societies*, Encounter Books, New York, 2008.
12 For more on conceptual relativism, see Roger Trigg, *Reason and Commitment*, Cambridge University Press, Cambridge, 1973, pp. 14–26.
13 See Roger Trigg, *Understanding Social Science*, 2nd ed., Basil Blackwell, Oxford, 2001, chapter 4.

a shared human nature brings, as what counts as natural and human varies from society to society and from conceptual system to conceptual system.

Relativism dooms us to ethnocentricity. Yet the very statement of relativism gives an apparent lie to this ethnocentricity. Even if it is granted that our way of seeing the world is different from that of others, and even if we all live according to the standards of different religions, saying that truth is relative to different conceptual systems seems to assume that at some point we can see that all such systems are different, and that they each do have different standards of truth and meaning. In denying any objective reality, the relativist still seems to be asserting the existence of a reality in which there are objective differences between cultures and systems of belief.

The idea of different conceptual systems has to be a nonrelativistic notion. The relativists could qualify such claims by saying that they are themselves relative to the conceptual system of the relativist, and should be understood accordingly. This assumes that those outside a system can still understand it, and that has to be one of the points at issue. Even so, any rational acceptance of the position is still impossible. If reasons, as it is said, gain their life within systems and do not have any life apart from them, then they cannot be offered except as a rhetorical device, as a serious way of convincing those outside the relativist's own system of belief.

The argument between proponents and opponents of realism formed one of the major controversies in the philosophy of religion in the last quarter of the twentieth century. The issue was precipitated by the reactions to the logical positivism and verificationism already mentioned. Applying a science-based philosophy to religion proved catastrophic, and all religious views seemed in need of reinterpretation for them to still hold. The accusation of total meaninglessness proved hard to shake off, even though in the end the hard-edged verificationism being put forward proved to be a bad account of science itself. It was incapable of dealing with the theoretical entities of science.[14]

14 See Roger Trigg, *Rationality and Science: Can Science Explain Everything?* Blackwell, Oxford, 1993.

LANGUAGE IN CONTEXT

In this context, the philosophy of the later Wittgenstein was very influential. Wittgenstein had even been associated with the science-based philosophy of the Vienna Circle in his earlier days, but reacted very strongly against any idea that language gets its meaning in any one way, perhaps through naming an objective reality. Instead, he came to see language as embedded in the social contexts of different ways of life and intimately linked with human practices. In his brief "Lectures on Religious Belief," this view comes out very clearly.[15] For example he says: "Whether a thing is a blunder or not – it is a blunder in particular system. Just as something is a blunder in a particular game and not in another."[16]

Wittgenstein was very fond of referring to language-games and to using games as an analogy. Games are rule-governed activities in which one is distinct from another. Thus, one cannot use the standards of one game to judge another: it is against the rules (except for a few exceptions) to handle a ball in soccer, but not in rugby. Another facet of games is that they are practices, and Wittgenstein saw the use of language as woven into the way we acted. Meaning was use, and it was its context in practice that formed it. This broke religion away from the straitjacket of science-orientated philosophy. The standards of science belonged in one game, and those of religion could be in another.

Another favorite notion of his is that of a "form of life."[17] At this point, however, things become unclear. There is a clear antirealist, even relativist tendency in Wittgenstein's later thought. Yet the way he, and those philosophers who seized on his views, used the concept often left it fuzzy on how one form of life was to be distinguished from another. If basic disagreement is a symptom of the existence of different forms of life, then religious language is not just different from scientific language, but each religion is separated into its own conceptual scheme too. The result was that those philosophers who felt that religion could

15 Ludwig Wittgenstein, *Lectures and Conversations on Aesthetics, Psychology and Religious Belief*, ed. Cyril Barrett, Blackwell, Oxford, 1966.
16 Wittgenstein, *Lectures and Conversations*, p. 59.
17 See Trigg, *Reason and Commitment*, chapter 4, and Trigg, *Rationality and Religion: Does Faith Need Reason*, chapter 7.

be justified philosophically on its own terms soon found that they were in danger of losing any grip on the notion of truth. Indeed a worst-case scenario was that although religion could no longer be seen as meaningless but should be accepted according to its own lights, it ceded any claim to truth to science, which thus still held the high ground from an epistemological point of view.

Yet that did not do justice to Wittgenstein's own views. He was averse to the idea that religion claimed "facts." He dismissed the idea that a historical basis for Christianity could provide a rational justification, even if there was indubitable evidence. He said that was "because the indubitability wouldn't be enough to make me change my whole life."[18] Yet he generalized from this position and viewed science itself as in a similar position of being a system that could not claim any external justification, but could proceed according to its own internal rules. In some of his latest thought, captured in notebooks in the last year or so before his death in 1951, his thinking was very clearly relativist.[19] He tackled the issue of whether physics itself could proclaim its truth in the teeth of opposition, for instance from people who believed in oracles instead. He said of consulting oracles in this way: "If we call this 'wrong' aren't we using our language-game as a base from which to combat theirs?"[20] We are using the rules of one system to attack what goes in another, just as if I complained about a football match that not enough runs were being scored, or about a cricket match that I had not seen a single home run.

This idea that the truth and the facts are constituted by the system and have a life within it, but no validity beyond, may put religion and science on a par. Wittgenstein is resolutely opposed to the idea that human rationality, and the giving of reasons, can somehow float free of the particular context in human life in which they gained their life. The slogan "meaning is use," which summarizes his approach, reiterates how our words and the whole language we use are embedded in our practices and ways of living. Some of these may relate to our position as human beings. He remarks at one point that "what we are supplying are

18 Wittgenstein, *Lectures and Conversations*, p. 57.
19 For more on this, see Trigg, *Reason and Commitment*.
20 Ludwig Wittgenstein, *On Certainty*, ed. G. E. M. Anscombe, and G. H. von Wright, Blackwell, Oxford, 1969, #609.

really remarks on the natural history of human beings."[21] Yet his later work suggests a willingness to relate the giving of reasons to different belief systems. In the context of religion, that might suggest a willingness to see religious differences as evidence of a difference in language-games and forms of life. Different religions may simply be different systems of belief with no common ground, and thus are incommensurable.

According to Wittgenstein, words and their meanings cannot be prised apart from their practical context. Further, we should not look for explanations but simply note the game and say "this language-game is played."[22] To revert to his example of the people who resist physics but believe in oracles, he maintains that we cannot rationally criticize them. He significantly says that "at the end of reasons comes persuasion" and comments darkly: "think what happens when missionaries convert natives."[23] Wittgenstein was very alert to the issue of the justification of religious belief and said in the end that it may be justified within its own terms, but it cannot appeal to any justification that appealed to a free-floating rationality or any idea of objective truth. Such concepts are constructed out of the way we use our language in the course of living our lives. It seemed to be his eventual position that different ways of life, "forms of life," will generate different standards of truth and meaning. The implication of his remark about missionaries was that different religions were themselves only to be justified in their own terms.

Indeed, in remarks made about accounts of "primitive" religion and magic, by the Scottish anthropologist Sir James Frazer in his famous 1922 book on magic and religion, Wittgenstein was very contemptuous of the way Frazer makes the magical and religious notions of the people he was studying "mistakes." Frazer had attempted in *The Golden Bough* to map a progress from magic to religious belief and then scientific belief. He was particularly influenced by the story of the pre-Roman priest-king of Nemi in Italy, who was ritually murdered by his successor. However, Wittgenstein complains that when Frazer attempts to explain rituals, such as the killing of a priest-king, all that he does is "make this

21 Wittgenstein, *Philosophical Investigations I* #415, trans G. E. M. Anscombe, Blackwell, Oxford, 1958.
22 Wittgenstein, *Philosophical Investigations*, #655.
23 *On Certainty*, #612.

practice plausible to people who think as he does."[24] In other words, he is appealing to his own system of belief, but in the process misrepresents what he claims to be describing. He just sees magic as a faulty way of trying to get things done.

Wittgenstein's basic position was that it is a mistake to represent religious practices as resting on wrong beliefs. He decried the fact that, as he sees it, Frazer represents people as stupid for believing certain things. Wittgenstein argued that it may be all very well "when you can make a man change his way of doing things simply by calling his attention to his error." Wittgenstein continued: "This is not how it is in connection with the religious practices of a people; and what we have here is *not* an error."[25] It only makes sense within the particular context of their way of life and practices. Frazer's explanation for why a rainmaking ceremony persists, even if it is actually ineffective, is because it will eventually be followed by rain and then might appear effective. Wittgenstein thought it very implausible that people are simply stupid or irrational.

As some philosophers have claimed, there is no "God's-eye view," from which we can survey the scene as it looks from the outside of all conceptual schemes, theories, or ways of life.[26] We are all situated somewhere and see things from a particular viewpoint. There is an obvious truth about this. It is like demanding that someone who has poor eyesight take their spectacles off to check whether the world looks the same as with the spectacles. That person needs their help to see in the first place. That of itself, however, does not prove that somehow the spectacles are constructing the world, and that things are not as they appear. Conceptual schemes may be better or worse at capturing reality, just as some spectacles may be more helpful in giving sharp vision.

The later Wittgenstein had no truck with any idea of a world as it was in and of itself, or a pure rationality that could somehow be related to the way things are, let alone with the notion that *we* see things as they are and others do not. Again and again he reverted to the idea that we can only describe and not use philosophy as a way of judging. As

---

24 Ludwig Wittgenstein, *Remarks on Frazer's Golden Bough*, ed. Rush Rhees, Brynmill, Retford, 1979, p. 2.
25 Wittgenstein, *Remarks on Frazier's Golden Bough*, p. 2.
26 See Trigg, *Rationality and Science*, chapter 5.

he said in the *Philosophical Investigations*: "I shall get burnt if I put my hand in the fire: that is certainty. That is to say: here we have the meaning of certainty."[27] In other words, even such a philosophically loaded term gets its meaning from our basic practices, and is not to be rationally connected with some metaphysical structure.

UNDERSTANDING ALIEN PRACTICES

Wittgenstein pursues this in connection with religious practices, even those that were thought by many to be primitive. He says that "we can only describe and say human life is like that."[28] Thus religious symbols are used in the course of a way of life but are not to be understood to rest on an opinion that could be at error.[29] He explicitly links his views of the interpretation of "primitive" religion with modern understandings of religion, saying that the kind of actions referred to by Frazer "are not different in kind from any genuinely religious action today, say a confession of sins." His view is that we can make clear what is happening but not "explain it in some quasi-scientific manner."[30] Magic, according to Wittgenstein, expresses a wish and is not just an ignorant attempt to manipulate the world.

There remains a large caveat that Wittgenstein makes explicit, but which begins to cast doubt even on our ability to "describe" in the way he suggests. He refers to the danger of "identifying one's own gods with the gods of other peoples," so that, as he says, "one becomes convinced that the names have the same meaning."[31] In other words, we tend to project our own understandings, and indeed our own conceptual scheme, on that of others which may be very different. Wittgenstein illustrates this in a devastating remark about the way a "priest" is to be understood. He claims: "Frazer cannot imagine a priest who is not basically an English parson of our times with all his stupidity and feebleness."[32]

Our propensity to see even the way other people see things in our own terms can be just a psychological difficulty. We naturally judge

27 Wittgenstein, *Philosophical Investigations*, #474.
28 Wittgenstein, *Remarks on Frazer's Golden Bough*, p. 3.
29 See Wittgenstein, *Remarks on Frazier's Golden Bough*, p. 3.
30 Wittgenstein, *Remarks on Frazier's Golden Bough*, p. 4.
31 Wittgenstein, *Remarks on Frazier's Golden Bough*, p. 8.
32 Wittgenstein, *Remarks on Frazier's Golden Bough* p. 5.

the world according to how we have experienced it, and we may find it difficult not just to empathize with those who are alien, but even to comprehend how they see things. We project our own concepts onto their understanding, and in the process misrepresent them. For someone familiar with the talk of the Christian God, it may be a fundamental mistake to assume that a god or gods referred to in different contexts are fundamentally similar. The features of the alien society may not be easily compared with our own society. Some "primitive" cult may have its priests, perhaps even administering a fertility cult. To see them as fulfilling the same role as the vicar of an English country parish is a total misunderstanding.

These are salutary reminders that are important issues in both the philosophy of religion and the philosophy of social science.[33] Ethnocentricity, being so rooted in our own way of life that we simply project our conceptual scheme onto that of others, can lead us to see similarities when there are none. It can lead to a lack of sympathy, so that other societies are judged by our own standards and inevitably found lacking. This can be particularly so with religion because it is both central to the understanding of alien societies and formative in forming our own views, whether we fully realize it or not. The attempts to counteract all of this in the study of other cultures leads to a stress on the importance of fieldwork in anthropology, to see how another society functions from the point of view of the participants.

Wittgenstein saw concepts as intimately linked with language, so that they were socially shared and rooted in context. This is why he famously found the idea of a "private language" incomprehensible, and why he found it difficult to conceive of private apprehensions of God, independent of any social and linguistic context of teaching. We all, he thought, enter into systems of belief that are social in character and not the construction of individuals. His ideas about the nature of concepts found favor in particular with those who stressed the role of society over the individual.

In a political context, some Marxists saw a commonality between their thinking and that of Wittgenstein. In the religious context, his ideas were seized on by some Roman Catholics, with their stress on

---

33 See, for example, Trigg *Understanding Social Science*, chapter 4.

the corporate nature of the Church, as opposed to it being a voluntary assembly of individuals coming together to share beliefs that had
been arrived at independently. Wittgenstein was very unsure of a report
about a deaf-mute from William James who had written that "in his
[the deaf-mute's] early youth, even before he could speak, he had had
thoughts about God and the world." Wittgenstein was dismissive of
this as "a queer memory phenomenon, from which he could draw
no conclusions."[34] To him, all language, to be meaningful, had to be
anchored in a shared public world. Otherwise we could not use the
same concepts and communicate with each other.

Religions were social and in part constitutive of what Wittgenstein at
times called a "form of life." He claimed that "what has to be accepted,
the given, is so one could say – forms of life" (Lebensformen in the
German original.)[35] They cannot be justified in terms of anything else,
but are the starting point for understanding. Yet that raises a question
about how one form of life can be understood from the standpoint of
another. How can we avoid total incomprehension of different cultures
and religions? We may see them only in our own terms, and that will
lead to total misrepresentation. Are we doomed, from a conceptual
standpoint, to perpetual mutual misunderstanding?

This became a pressing problem in the philosophy of religion. At
first, the stress on the different uses of language and the need to accept
them in their own terms seemed like a release from the straitjacket of
verificationism and rigid science-based philosophy. Religion could be
accepted on its own terms. However, once it was seen that it was not
just a matter of the difference between religion and science, but of the
difference between religions and ways of life, the problems mounted.
Wittgenstein explicitly related the idea of agreement as the basis of the
notion of a form of life.[36] He went on to say that "if language is to
be a means of communication there must be agreement not only in
definitions but also (queer as this may sound) in judgments."[37]

This means that as judgments diverge, together with the practices in
which they are bound up, our ability to communicate will break down.

34 Wittgenstein, *Philosophical Investigations*, #342.
35 Wittgenstein, *Philosophical Investigations*, II xi, p. 226.
36 Wittgenstein, *Philosophical Investigations*, #241.
37 Wittgenstein, *Philosophical Investigations*, #242.

It seems as if different forms of life construct their own conceptual systems. We are each rooted in our own system and cannot come to grips with those of others. There is nothing outside those systems against which they can be calibrated. Wittgenstein himself seemed to toy with the idea that a common human nature gave us such a basis. His growing stress, however, on the importance of an agreement in judgments as a basis for commonality meant that this idea had to recede. Human reactions may be similar in similar situations, but the way they are conceptualized may significantly differ.

RELIGIOUS REALITY

The followers of Wittgenstein's later philosophy on religion made it seem as if there could be no common basis for different religions. The influential Welsh philosopher, D. Z. Phillips, attacked theological realism, the idea that religion concerns an objective reality (perhaps God) that existed independently of the different beliefs and practices of different religions. This notion of reality floating free of the context in which reference to it made sense was anathema to him. In one of his earlier books he distinguished his view from that of those like Braithwaite who saw pictures in religion as mere psychological aids. For Phillips, as for Wittgenstein, the whole weight was in the picture. He complained that otherwise "it is as if one had a notion of truth apart from the pictures, by appeal to which they are measured."[38] For Phillips that was impossible.

Phillips dubbed it an "error of thinking" to assume that distinctions between truth and falsity stand in need of what he termed "an external guarantee such as God." He maintained that "the criteria of truth and falsity are internally related to the contexts in question." That is not a bad definition of relativism: there is no such thing as truth away from particular, and no doubt differing, contexts. Truth is constituted with "internal relations" rather than being constituted with a connection to something "external."[39] The idea excluded the sense being given to ideas of God apart from the particular and differing social contexts that gave them life, and hence meaning.

38 D. Z. Phillips, *Death and Immortality*, Macmillan, London, 1970, p. 77.
39 D. Z. Phillips, *The Concept of Prayer*, Routledge and Kegan Paul, London, 1965, p. 22.

Realism, in the context of religion, is the philosophical thesis about the relation of God, gods, or any other transcendent entity to religious belief. Such beliefs are justified or unjustified insofar as they succeed or fail in referring to a reality that exists independently of the belief. Atheists can be realists, and indeed have to be because they say that a religious belief cannot be justified. Realism concerns metaphysical possibility, something that Phillips, following Wittgenstein, cannot allow. The idea of believing something to be true seemingly cannot be given any sense apart from the practices that give them life. Phillips sums up his position by writing: "When the theological realist seeks to divorce the meaning of believing from our actions and practices, he effects a divorce between belief and practice which would render any kind of believing unintelligible."[40] We cannot refer to anything outside the concrete social contexts that gave such language its role.

Social contexts vary considerably, as do religions. Each is internally constructed by a social practice. We are mired in a relativism that forbids us from saying that other religions are mistaken because they have mistaken views about what is true. Some might see that as a gain because it confronts a dangerous triumphalism in religion. However, it also becomes impossible even to understand one form of life, or language-game, from the standpoint of another. Each is judged in its own terms, but that inevitably means that those who are external to the practices cannot properly understand them. All religions become closed books to non-adherents. We cannot even compare different practices, or religions. Wittgenstein's approach means that the very idea of comparative religion is a mistake, just as ranking a religion as primitive has to be wrong. Indeed, to many, both within and beyond anthropology, the notion of a primitive religion wrongly suggests that there are external standards to be invoked that can justify the judgment.

The view is reminiscent of the views in the 1960s of Thomas Kuhn, who in reaction to positivism made much of the priority of theory in science. Different theories posited different entities and that meant, as he said, that such theories were "incommensurable."[41] None could be true, except by its own standards. The same trouble afflicts any view that

---

40 D. Z. Phillips, *Wittgenstein and Religion*, Macmillan, Basingstoke, 1993, p. 40.
41 See T. S. Kuhn, *The Structure of Scientific Revolutions*, University of Chicago Press, Chicago, 1962.

gives up any idea that there is a reality outside all human conceptions of it, against which our beliefs can in principle be measured. All we are left with are different systems of human concepts with no way of building bridges between them.

The philosophy of the later Wittgenstein ensured that religions could only be accepted on their own terms. The paradox is that such acceptance seems strictly impossible from an external standpoint. One joins a form of life, such as a religion, and participates in its practices and language, or one remains outside and finds it incomprehensible to a greater or lesser degree. In social anthropology, when similar views are adopted, the choice seems to be between joining a society and "going native" in order to understand, or remaining outside and not understanding but projecting our own views on it. The idea of a dispassionate and comparative social science seems in jeopardy.[42]

Such a position undermines the possibility of studying religions and makes the possibility of dialogue between religions appear impossible. What common ground is there to share for those committed to different religions if they cannot compare their different visions of a common reality? They cannot assume that they share a common human nature, because the concept of being human is constructed very differently in different forms of life. Unless we can all be understood as fundamentally sharing the same nature and similar reactions to a reality in which we are all situated, there can be little commonality between us. Much human contact across cultures is put at risk.

It may seem tolerant to want to understand other religions in their own terms, but without the idea of anything external to the beliefs, and not constructed by them, such understanding itself is illusory. Moreover, if others cannot be mistaken in their religious beliefs, neither can I, unless perhaps I am not obeying the common rules of the practice in which I participate. Yet if religions are not to be understood as making claims about a reality beyond them, then there can be no role for a proper humility, or a realization that our knowledge is limited. We are all epistemologically locked in separate compartments of belief, which are impervious to any notion of any external rational standards.

Wittgenstein is right to stress how religious beliefs are set in the context of people's whole life and are not just intellectual fancies set

42 See Trigg, *Reason and Commitment.*

apart from any of our practices. Religious beliefs – and, for example, particular moral practices – are very closely bound together. Even so, ways of life should rest on some conception of how the world is. Participants in religions typically see their beliefs as making assertions about the character of reality that, if mistaken, could undermine their belief. The philosophers who follow Wittgenstein, such as Phillips, say that religious believers often do not understand the "grammar" of their language. They think their language is doing one thing when it is being used in another way. Believers may be instinctive theological realists but are judged to be wrong in understanding their religious belief in that way. This seems a paradoxical view. We cannot, we are told, appeal to some objective reality, but have to accept language-games as "given." We have to participate to understand. Yet philosophers can, it seems, see what is actually going on in a language-game in a manner participants cannot. They can appeal to one kind of reality, while religious believers cannot appeal to another. Perhaps this is merely a practice in one philosophical form of life, but it is still one that purports to describe a reality in ways that have been said to be impossible.

The work of the later Wittgenstein has had an enormous influence on analytical philosophy and beyond. His ideas have even fed into the wider movement of postmodernism, which also stresses the importance of traditions and different perspectives that can only be seen in their own terms. Yet without the conception of an objective reality as a goal or target, we are treading the short path to nihilism. The idea of a reality that humans are trying to understand, and that may give sense to our lives, is part of the very lifeblood of all religions. It is the antithesis of nihilism. Religion makes claims about an objective reality that holds for us all whether or not we are able or willing to recognize it. Its seriousness and importance has to depend on that.

3

RELIGIOUS PLURALISM

DIVINE REALITY AND TRUTH

Claiming that reality – any reality – is of a particular nature immediately excludes rival views from being true. Once something is said to be true, alternatives are ruled out. If I say it is raining, I cannot reasonably say it is not. A major function of language should be to communicate states of affairs to others. Assertions must concern truth, and they carry with them implicit denials. Otherwise, language may become not much more than a series of inarticulate sounds, like groans. The verificationists thought religious language was like that precisely because they thought that proper language should communicate truths and identify falsehoods. They needed evidence from the senses to decide which was which, and religious language seemed impervious to that.

That narrowed the idea of truth and falsehood, as well as the concept of meaning that they tied to those notions, in an arbitrary manner. However, the later Wittgenstein's solution was, in a sense, worse. By tying our ideas of reality to the difference such beliefs make in our lives, he was led to accept that there may be in effect as many "realities" as there are identifiable ways of life. D. Z. Phillips claims that realism distorts the "natural setting" of belief.[1] For him, the sense of religious beliefs "is not given independently of the mode of projection in which they have their natural home." What we mean depends on how we live. This is why for Phillips the idea of "really believing" is more important than believing what is real. The sense of the latter can only

---

1 "On Really Believing," in D. Z. Phillips, *Wittgenstein and Religion*, Macmillan, Basingstoke, 1993, p. 53.

be given by the use of terms embedded in our actions. We can never have wrong beliefs about what is real, because the latter has no independent existence. Belief and practice can never be prized apart. Whether we really believe and are sincere in our practices is one thing, but we cannot be proven wrong by "reality" being brandished in front of us. One cannot sever belief from its "object," because, as Phillips claims, "realism ignores the context in which the relation between belief and its object has its sense."[2]

The result is that philosophers can tell believers that they do not believe what they think they do. An apparently neutral philosophical analysis, recounting in Wittgenstein's terms the "grammar of concepts," can tell believers that they are not talking about "a Being," namely God. God is not an object but not much more than a concept learned in the process of participating in one possible way of life among many. A relativist philosophy may, it appears both say that there cannot be objective truth and also deny that conventional religious beliefs are correct. It seems that even relativism has to exclude some possibilities if it is to say anything at all.

Neither the scientistic dismissal of all religion as meaningless nor the acceptance of all religious forms of life proved viable. The former could not in consistency even talk of the falsity of religion. The latter found it could not agree with ordinary believers' accounts of their beliefs. Both made any rational examination of religious claims impossible. Yet religious claims tend of their nature to be realist. Their holders make claims about the nature of reality that may be well or poorly founded. That may lead to a strong commitment shown in collective ways of life and individual devotion, but it depends on ideas about a reality that is normally transcendent. It seems to go beyond our ability as humans to comprehend it fully. It may, indeed, encompass a life beyond death and a world beyond space and time.

We shall see in the next chapter how the cognitive science of religion demonstrates that tendencies to understand the world in this way are deeply rooted in human nature.[3] That does not prove that such

---

2 Phillips, *Wittgenstein and Religion*, p. 55.
3 See, for instance, Justin Barrett, *Why Would Anyone Believe in God?* Alta Mira Press, Lanham, MD, 2004, and Justin Barrett, *Cognitive Science, Religion, and Theology: From Human Minds to Divine Minds*, Templeton Press, West Conshohocken, PA, 2011.

tendencies are reliable, but impulses toward religious belief are intimately connected with the whole cognitive architecture of the human mind. This apparently universal feature of the human mind, constantly attested to by anthropologists, gives the lie to the understanding, encouraged by conceptual relativism, that we are all parceled up into separate compartments unable to understand each other. There may be more of a common conceptual base than is sometimes realized, stemming from a more substantial human nature than used to be admitted.[4]

What sense can be given then to the idea of a divine reality accessible to everyone? Does not the mere existence of so many different religions give the lie to that idea? When beliefs diverge and conflict, choices between them can seem arbitrary or even result in a preference for the familiar. If we were born in Canterbury, Kent, we are likely to be Christian, and in Baghdad, Muslim. Our background will determine what we find acceptable, or so philosophers like to suggest.

Nevertheless, truth still appears to be at stake. We may, if we are Christian, accept the doctrine of the Trinity. If we are Muslim, we certainly will not. Both religions accept the idea of one God in a way that polytheists would not. Yet either Christ was a unique revelation of God, and even God Himself, or he was not. In the same way, either God is Creator of the world or, as Buddhists would hold, there is no such thing as "creation." Religions contradict each other. That is why they are different. We cannot get away from that awkward fact.

Are "we" right, and "they" wrong? The alternative to this dogmatic assertion might seem to be that there is no such thing as right and wrong, and that we have our way of life and they have theirs. Perhaps, as R. B. Braithwaite indicated, we agree about many ethical matters but entertain different inspirational stories. The philosopher of religion John Hick thought that there was another way. He wanted to respect the diversity of religions without giving up the idea that they all attempt to reveal something of the same reality. Assuming that, in the words of Joseph Runzo, "religious realism is the view that there is a transcendent divine reality independent of human thought,"[5] can we be religious

---

4 For more on these themes, see Roger Trigg, *Understanding Social Science: A Philosophical Introduction to the Social Sciences*, 2nd ed., Blackwell, Oxford, 2001.
5 Joseph Runzo, ed., *Is God Real?* Macmillan, Basingstoke, 1993, p. xiii.

realists, without simply calling those who disagree with us "fools and heretics"?

Religious realism may appear to imply that a transcendent reality is just as we think it is and, for example, that God's nature is as we conceive it. If this is put in terms of the collective beliefs of one religion, one might conclude that the Christian God is real and that Christian beliefs are correct in what they affirm. However, the same argument could also establish the truth of an alternative religion. There seems to be then little difference between that and relativism, or anti-realism, which simply says that the Christian God is real for Christians, and other gods may be real for others. A belief in a reality cannot itself be self-authenticating. Yet the point of realism is that those who believe in a particular reality do not just think that it is true for them. In the case of Christianity, the assumption – articulated or not – is that the Christian God exists, and those who do not acknowledge that assumption are just plain wrong. As nothing could be more important than the acknowledgment of the existence of a Creator, this can give rise to missionary activity and proselytizing. The motivation will be even stronger if people believe that the eternal destiny of others is at stake. It is a matter of "salvation."

The problem could be that, in holding that they are right, religions may be antagonistic to those who disagree and regard other religions as dangerous purveyors of falsehood. Believers could be less likely to listen to participants of other religions, let alone enter into dialogue with them. Hick dubs as "naive religious realism the idea that divine reality is literally just as spoken about in the language of one tradition."[6] This idea parallels a theory of naive realism in perception that holds that things are just as we perceive them to be. Such a view may have some superficial attraction in perceiving the everyday world, although even then it cannot account for perceptual illusions, such as a stick appearing bent in water.

Naive religious realism goes hand in hand in some people's eyes with the kind of certainty claimed by "fundamentalists" in religion. Naive realists in sense perception want to base epistemological theory on a secure empirical foundation, and the quest for foundations is always

6 John Hick, *An Interpretation of Religion: Human Responses to the Transcendent,* Macmillan, Basingstoke, 1989, p. 174.

present in epistemology. Without a certain starting point or base, the argument goes, we can have no guarantee of the truth of what we believe. In the same way, in religion, some look to a certainty guaranteed by inerrant truth, perhaps of a text, such as the Bible or the Qu'ran or perhaps by the authority of an institution, such as the Roman Catholic Church. The quest for truth seems to demand infallibility and certainty.

Making truth the product of people's beliefs or ways of life gets things the wrong way around. It produces different "truths" and "realities," and thus splits communities and religions off from each other with no possibility of any common ground. Realism tries to counteract this by insisting that the reality that is the target of our beliefs does not depend on us. Any anthropocentric theory linking reality to a human capability of finding it out must be the antithesis of theological realism. God is the prime example of a category of existence that could never be dependent on our understanding. By definition, God created us, not the other way around. Yet because that is so, naive realism itself begins to look very simpleminded. God is by definition so far beyond our understanding that the issue must surely be not about obtaining certainty about divine reality. The question is whether we can know anything at all about "it," or "Him," or however God is to be described.

A proper metaphysical realism that insists on the ontological independence and "self-subsistence" of whatever reality we are trying to refer to must then raise the question of how it can be known. By placing a logical distance between reality and those who conceptualize it, questions arise as to not only how we can be sure that our beliefs are right, but even whether we can ever know anything at all. Why should concepts and reality coincide? That is the ever-present threat of skepticism. It may seem a footling philosophical worry to be concerned about the reality of tables and chairs. It does not seem so extravagant when faced with issues about the reality of God, particularly when there is so much disagreement about whether there is one God, many gods, or none at all.

Religious realism could produce the kind of doubt that is corrosive of all religious belief. Religion of its nature is not just a matter of theoretical assent; it also demands personal commitment.[7] This is one

---

7 See Roger Trigg, *Reason and Commitment*, Cambridge University Press, Cambridge, 1973.

of the issues that lays behind the Wittgensteinian rejection of realism. Religious faith is not like entertaining a hypothesis but instead involves our lives. On the one hand, therefore, certainty seems to be the lifeblood of a religious life. On the other hand, it assumes a knowledge that it seems doubtful we can attain.

CRITICAL REALISM

Hick suggests that instead of a naive realism, what is needed is a modified form of realism, a "critical realism," which takes into account human limitations and cultural influences. He writes: "A critical religious realism affirms the transcendent divine reality which the theistic religions refer to as God, but is conscious that this reality is always thought and experienced by us in ways that are shaped and coloured by human concepts and images."[8]

Hick goes on to talk of this reality as "the Real," and he stresses that religious categories will differ significantly from culture to culture. This characterization accepts that religions are about something and claim truth, but they are also profoundly influenced by the cultures from which they spring. He tries to keep hold of the idea of reality as a guiding principle, but he acknowledges the way that different forms of human understanding actively influence our interpretation of that reality. His problem – from a philosophical point of view – is whether he can avoid the contrasting dangers of skepticism and relativism. Separating reality too much from our understanding invites the former. Making it too close to different understandings produces the latter.

Critical realism appears to confuse ideas of ontology and epistemology. Realism, as we have portrayed it, has to be a metaphysical notion about the status of reality. It is discovered, not constructed. Yet when Hick brings in factors about the ways in which culture and other factors shape our understanding, the problem becomes an epistemological one about how we can build up knowledge of the world. The nature of reality seems to be confused with the way we are compelled by our situation to think about it. Once it is accepted that others build up different conceptions of it, such as those given in different religions, we

8 "Religious Realism and Non-Realism: Defining the Issue," in Runzo, ed., *Is God Real?*. p. 7.

must give an account of how, even so, they are all somehow aiming at the same reality.

Do different religions talk of the same God? Given that their beliefs vary, are they aiming in the same direction? This is a perennial issue to which we shall return. In philosophical terms the question is how far the meaning, or sense, of a belief or term can be separated from its referent. If beliefs construct reality, the clear answer is that the referent must change according to the content of belief. Different beliefs are simply about different things, since those beliefs construct those things, and they are incommensurable. If, however, different beliefs all concern the same reality, all may, in principle, be compared in terms of their greater or lesser success in capturing that reality. Who is to decide? Given that none of us has a "God's-eye view," perhaps only God can, but whose God? We appear to have solved nothing.

"Exclusivists" have been defined as those who say that only one religious tradition is right and purveys truth. That may rule out the possibility that other religions can recognize any truth at all, but we all know that many religions overlap in their assertions. Christians, Jews, and Muslims all agree that there is one God, although there can be arguments about whether they are worshipping "the same God." If we acknowledge that different religions can recognize the same truth and can have shared beliefs about it, one may adopt an "inclusivist" position by saying that other religions can claim truth but that ours sets the standard. In other words, we can see the good in other religions insofar as they are treading the same path as we are. Some, such as the theologian Karl Rahner, have been tempted to say that such people can be Christians without knowing it. He calls them "anonymous Christians." That seems highly patronizing toward people who may be good and sincere and have still deliberately rejected Christianity. The idea that "we know best" seems to be trumpeted. Yet people in other religions can play the same game and say that their own beliefs set the standard.

Arguments about exclusivism and inclusivism can become highly technical, raising questions as to precisely what is meant.[9] One broad distinction is that the argument can be both about truth and about

9 See, for instance, the careful analysis in Robert McKim, *On Religious Diversity*, Oxford University Press, New York, 2012.

salvation. Does only one religion possess truth? Can adherents of all religions be "saved," whatever is meant by that word? A strong tradition in Christian thinking holds that questions about salvation are a matter for God alone. John Wesley, for instance, thought that Christians could not claim scriptural authority to decide who could be saved.[10] The issue of truth can be treated separately. What is true and whether others can be held responsible for not believing it are distinct questions. Perhaps only an omniscient and perfectly just God can properly judge the latter issue. Limited human beings cannot.

Objecting to exclusivism about truth because it rules out some positions brings us back to the fact that there has to be a difference between saying that something is so and saying that it is not. Asserting anything at all has to rule out alternatives. If anything goes, that is the end of language. Religious language is not alone in excluding possibilities. When anyone tries to communicate anything, that is what they are doing.

Even so, the fear is that, in religion, exclusivism breeds intolerance. Hick puts forward an idea of *pluralism*, which accepts that all religions (or, at least, many) were equally valid. Different religions are on an equal footing in the pursuit of truth. This is not relativism because, for Hick, there is a reality, the Real, to be sought. Furthermore, the pluralist makes claims about its nature in that it cannot be as one religion says it is. Ideas of the Christian God may provide one form of response to the Real, but it is not the only possible one and certainly not a definitive one.

Can one retain a realist perspective and yet accept that religions are on an epistemological par? They may contradict each other, so how can we know anything about divine reality? The response Hick gives owes much to the philosophy of Kant. The latter draws a distinction between things as they are "in themselves," the *noumena*, and things as they appear to us, the *phenomena*. That, for Hick, is not just a statement about human limitations because he takes it a step further by accepting that different cultural influences produce different "appearances." Because none of us has access to reality "in itself," its nature will appear to differ according to our cultural and religious situations. The Real appears in different religions in different guises, or, as Hick

---

10 See McKim, *On Religious Diversity*, p. 73.

claims, different *personae* and *impersonae*.[11] It is not even personal or impersonal in itself.

What features then does God have? All major religions attempt to describe His reality, and whatever we say will ally us with one religion rather than another. Even referring to "God" and to "Him" projects particular religious understanding on to what the ultimate divine reality is really like. Hick places the Real as "the postulated ground of the different forms of religious experience," but he thinks that none of our conceptual frameworks can be properly applied to it.[12] That would illegitimately cross the gap between the noumenal and the phenomenal. He even says that the Real as such "cannot be said to be one or many, person or thing, substance or process, good or evil, purposive or non-purposive."[13]

Hick is treading here a very fine line between relativism and realism. He claims he is a committed realist, asserting that there is a reality behind all appearances and, moreover, a reality that can ground hope. He says very emphatically that "the cosmic optimism of the great world faiths depends absolutely upon a realist interpretation of their language."[14] He explains this as follows in an important observation:

For it is only if this universe is the creation or expression of an ultimate over-arching benign reality, and is such that the spiritual project of our existence continues in some form beyond this present life, that it is possible to expect a fulfilment that can justify the immense pain and travail of the journey.

He adds that "a non-realist interpretation of religion inevitably entails a profound cosmic pessimism. . . . [It] abandon[s] hope for humankind as a whole."[15] Hick has in mind here issues arising from the problems of evil and suffering. Life for many, particularly those outside the affluent West, can be hard and short. It is tragic and pointless unless part of a larger whole. It is what St. Paul had in mind when he proclaimed the truth of Christ's resurrection and went on to say that "if it is for this life only that Christ has given us hope, we are of all people most to

11 Hick, *An Interpretation of Religion*, p. 246.
12 Hick, *An Interpretation of Religion*, p. 236.
13 Hick, *An Interpretation of Religion*, p. 246.
14 John Hick, "Realism versus non-Realism," in Runzo, ed., *Is God Real?*, p. 12.
15 Hick, "Realism versus non-Realism," p. 13.

be pitied."[16] The nature of many religions depends not on the entertainment of inspiring stories but on a belief that they point to objective truths about the eternal destiny of human beings. As Hick suggests, the alternative is pessimism and despair.

In proclaiming this religious hope, Hick is not presenting a neutral analysis of all possible religion. He is saying that the Real has a definite character that gives reason for hope. Yet that seems to go against his refusal to see it as having any definite character. However, he insists that differing insights from various religions can provide equally valid insights into the nature of the Real, together giving genuine understanding about the ultimate destiny of humans. He gives as examples notions such as "God, Brahman, Dharmakaya, rebirth, eternal life," all of which point to an ultimate "fulfilment that can justify the immense pain and travail of the journey."[17] He has in mind a fulfillment to be welcomed and a ground for present hope.

Hick's pluralism can be partly reconciled with his cosmic optimism because he restricts his attention to what he terms "the great world faiths."[18] He is looking to religions that provide contexts for salvation/liberation – namely, "the transformation of human existence from self-centredness to Reality-centredness."[19] He judges religion by the criterion of such "salvific transformation," resulting in moral fruits, "which can be identified by means of the ethical ideal, common to all the great traditions, of *agape/karunja* (love/compassion)." No doubt, the "great" religions do often overlap in their ethical ideals, and from the standpoint of each, there is good in the others. That, though, is an inclusive outlook that is normally contrasted with Hick's pluralism.

If one religion was correct in some of its identification of the Real, that would drag Hick back into an inclusivist position. Saying a group of religions, even the "great world faiths," concur in their optimism seems still to be a form of inclusivism. It certainly excludes some religions, such as devil worship. Even so, he tries to follow the implications of his Kantian distinction between the noumenal Real and the phenomenal Real as they are experienced by us. He says: "None of the concrete

16 I Corinthians 15, 19.
17 Hick, "Realism versus non-Realism," p. 13.
18 Hick, *An Interpretation of Religion*, p. 10.
19 Hick, *An Interpretation of Religion*, p. 300.

descriptions that apply within the realm of human experience can apply literally to the unexperienced ground of that realm."[20] This has great implications. Hick does not want any particular religion to be able to claim superiority of insight over others. It follows that the Real cannot be as any particular religion, or group of religions, says it is. The Real in itself must always be sharply distinguished from any of the ways it is conceptualized.

NEGATIVE THEOLOGY

This may seem to resonate with "negative theology," the view that stresses that we, as finite beings, cannot grasp the infinite nature of God, who is literally ineffable. Any view that points, as realism does, to the wholly "other" nature of the divine has to explain how the gap between the divine and the human can be bridged. As has been mentioned in the preceding chapter, Plato also confronts this philosophical point. His stress on "Forms" or "Ideas" as objectively real leads to the question of how we can obtain knowledge of them. His answer is that our souls were, in a previous form of existence, in contact with them, and we are led to "recollect" them through education in the circumstances of this life. Without some such story, there would be no conceivable way that knowledge of that kind of reality could be acquired.

Some religions do talk of reincarnation and different lives, but without that, some notion of revelation is essential. If we have not been in the presence of God or the Real, its nature has to be revealed to us in terms that are accessible to us as humans. Christianity speaks of God literally becoming human so that the divine can be revealed to us in the context of this life. John Hick, with his stress on the "myth" of the Incarnation, undercuts the possibility of this identification of Jesus with divinity. Once Christ is not identified with God but seen just as a prophet among others, one explanation of our ability to understand God within the terms of human life is removed. The question has to be asked as to whether He has been removed beyond our grasp.

It has been said of Hick's views that "his entirely ineffable Real more closely resembles an emptiness that is ineffable and beyond the scope of

---

20 Hick, *An Interpretation of Religion*, p. 246.

human concepts than it resembles a loving or a compassionate God."[21]
The more he tries to say that all or some religions converge on one
reality, the more he has to evacuate that reality of any characteristics
not accepted by one of those religions. The issue is what will be left.
Hick is overreaching by concentrating on religions with a strong ethical
component. He wants to replace self-centeredness with something else.
To give one example, he is not concerned with ritualistic religions, such
as those of the ancient Greeks and Romans, which paid little attention
to ethical behavior, let alone *agape*, or a love that looks suspiciously
Christian in conception.

Hick's reference to the "great traditions" suggests that, in dealing
with religion beyond his own Christian tradition, he still thinks that
"love" and "compassion" set a standard. Religions that do not tread a
soteriological path – those that turn us away from ourselves and toward
how things should be – are outside his remit. The darker side of religion
is ignored. Yet a genuine pluralist has to accept all conceptions of "the
Ultimate" as equally valid and cannot privilege any one set.

There is even a danger of circularity in Hick's identification of the
"great world faiths." He could be concentrating on those that fit in best
with what he himself wants to say about the Real. His assertion of "an
ultimate overarching benign reality" is in direct contradiction with his
previously quoted view that the Real in itself can be "neither good nor
evil, purposive or non-purposive."[22] We cannot, if that is right, use it
to ground any optimism or hope about the ultimate destiny of humans.
To do so would be to begin to conceptualize what, according to Hick,
must always lie beyond our conception.

Hick cannot decide what the relation of the Real is to our various
conceptual schemes. Some pluralists may want to contend that each
religion is holding on to one particular part of reality in a way that is
ultimately compatible with other insights. Hick's idea of the noumenal,
in contrast, seems to say that the noumenon is the causal ground of
different phenomena, but it also may be unrelated in character to any
of them. That is not the same as the picture of pluralism that is sometimes given in popular understandings of religion. The famous story,
originating in India, of the blind men and the elephant encapsulates the

21 McKim, *On Religious Diversity*, p. 116.
22 Hick, "Realism versus non-Realism," p. 12.

idea that one can grasp partial truth, even if one is not in a position to see the whole. One of the blind men felt the elephant's leg and thought he was beside a great pillar. Another felt the tail and thought it was a rope, whereas a third felt the elephant's trunk and thought it was the branch of a tree. A tusk appeared to be a solid pipe. In a sense, all were mistaken, at least in the descriptions they gave, but in another sense, they were all perceiving parts of a wider reality.

That is not the relation of the noumenal to the phenomenal. The former can only act as a regulative concept but still be strictly beyond our comprehension. We are not seeing bits of a wider whole. The reality is permanently hidden behind a veil that cannot be breached. If it could be, the Real could be said by us to have some characteristics. Hick says, however, that we can only make purely formal statements about it, as Anselm did when describing his view of God, or the divine reality, as "that than which nothing greater can be conceived."[23] The problem that Hick faces is exacerbated by the differences between religions. He is not simply referring to human inadequacy in confronting the infinite and in trying to comprehend it. That is an issue about transcendence and ineffability. He wants to legitimize different religions in the eyes of each other. He is accepting difference but trying to show its ultimate unimportance. None of them is better than the others, because none of them can gain any insight into the Real as it is.

Kant talks in his philosophy about the human condition and our inability as humans to break past the ways things appear to us.[24] Hick, on the other hand, also deals with disagreements between religions and cultures, accepting differences as, in some sense, ultimate. Although he explicitly challenges the anti-realism of the Wittgensteinians, his own critical realism appears to leave us without the ability to say anything with assurance about what ultimate reality is really like. Hick may accept that religious belief does have a target, or a regulative ideal. Yet his view of religion is similar to a game of soccer in which not only are no goals scored, but they cannot be. Even if the Real has a causal role in inspiring different religions, its nature is by definition never reflected in the beliefs of any of them or mirrored in any way of life that could

23 Hick, *An Interpretation of Religion*, p. 246.
24 See Roger Trigg, *Ideas of Human Nature: An Historical Introduction*, 2nd ed., Blackwell, Oxford, 1999, ch. 7.

be traced back to it as a source. Either the Real is personal or it is not. Either it is good or it is not. Because of the way that Hick has set up the divide between noumenal and phenomenal, there seems to be no way of deciding. If we could decide, we would probably be privileging the insights of one religion, or type of religion, over another.

Metaphysical realists – those who take seriously the independent reality of the divine – have to accept that, although there may be partial and imperfect access to the Real, it cannot be totally hidden from us. If it was, it would be difficult to keep to any meaningful form of realism. The idea that the noumenal has some causal influence itself becomes irrelevant from a conceptual point of view once it is accepted that there is no connection between the nature of the Real and how we conceptualize "it," whatever "it" may be. Some religions extol altruism, but that is only an interesting coincidence unless it can be taken that this somehow reflects the character of that reality. Some ancient views of causation assumed that like causes like, but that is not a modern view. The concept of the Real can quickly appear redundant, completely failing to explain either differences or similarities between beliefs.

In a different context, but still concerning the relation between concepts and reality, the later Wittgenstein agonizes about the application of concepts of sensation. He argues that all concepts have to be anchored in the public world and cannot name a "private object." This is part of his attempt to wean us away from thinking of concepts as names of things in the world. Trying to show that language functions in different ways, he suggests that if we insist on seeing the word "pain" as naming a private sensation, on the model of "object and designation," "the object drops out of consideration as irrelevant."[25] The private feeling, he claims, does not contribute to our shared understanding. Indeed, he goes on to affirm that "a nothing could serve just as well as a something about which nothing could be said."[26]

We do not have to follow Wittgenstein's views about the language of sensations to draw a wider philosophical conclusion. The idea of any form of reality can be important, giving us a sense of direction in our attempts to discover its nature. If, however, it is by definition

25 Ludwig Wittgenstein, *Philosophical Investigations*, trans. G. E. M. Anscombe, Blackwell, Oxford, 1958, #293.
26 Wittgenstein, *Philosophical Investigations*, #304.

inaccessible, can we be sure our language can engage with anything at all? Nothing can count against what we say, and that means that nothing can count in its favor either. There seems little point in saying anything. Realism like this seems no different in practice from the non-realism it opposes.

Kant's philosophy of noumena historically raised just this kind of problem. Once the problem becomes conceptual divergence and not just our similarity in reactions as human beings, it is easy for "the object" to drop out as irrelevant. After the emergence of types of idealism, which simply tie reality to human understanding, came a more radical reaction against the modernist ideas of reason, which were seen to be exemplified by Kant in the later Enlightenment. Postmodernism has gloried in the diversity of beliefs and traditions, taking them seriously as ultimate facts. It has denied any possibility of appealing to rationality to resolve differences. The step from skepticism about our ability to conceptualize the Real to an outright relativism can be short indeed.

THE EQUALITY OF RELIGIONS?

Hick's views have had an influence far beyond Anglo-American discussions of the philosophy of religion. Indeed, Cardinal Joseph Ratzinger, soon to become Pope Benedict XVI, singled Hick's views out for particular criticism in one of his books. Ratzinger calls him "a prominent representative of religious relativism, where the post-metaphysical philosophy of Europe converges in a remarkable way with the negative theology of Asia, for which the divinity can never enter, in itself and undisguised, into the world of appearances in which we live."[27] As Ratzinger explains it, the Divinity "only ever shows itself in relative reflections and in itself remains beyond all words and beyond all comprehension in absolute transcendence."

Yet, as we have just seen, the problem is whether, even by causal influence, the Divinity is at all "showing itself." If it is, we would be getting only partial glimpses of it, as the blind men did with the elephant. It remains unclear whether Hick allows that. He says that "we

---

27 Joseph Cardinal Ratzinger, *Truth and Tolerance: Christian Belief and World Religions*, Ignatius Press, San Francisco, 2004, p. 121.

cannot . . . say that the Real *an sich* has the characteristics of its manifestations, such as (in the case of the heavenly Father) love and justice
or (in the case of Brahman) consciousness and bliss."[28] Yet the Real is
the ground of these characteristics. Hick continues by saying: "In so far
as the heavenly Father and Brahman are two authentic manifestations
of the Real, the love and justice of the one and the consciousness and
bliss of the other are aspects of the Real as manifested within human
experience."

The problem is that Hick wants it both ways. No religion is allowed
to claim superiority over another, but he surreptitiously imports the
strongly ethical notion of a "salvific transformation" of human life. Yet
it is illegitimate for him to concentrate on those religions that encourage
turning away from self toward reality, since he wants to block the idea
that any particular religious faith has any superior knowledge with
which to judge other faiths. At the same time, he hankers after the idea
that some manifestations of the Real are "authentic." If some religions
are better than others in responding to the Real as it is, why might
not some, or even one, of those have a greater understanding than all
the rest? Given what Hick says, though, responses to the Real may be
merely effects produced by encountering it, and those in no way reveal
any of its nature.

It is not surprising that Ratzinger sees Hick as a post-metaphysical
relativist. We seem to be left with alternative claims about the nature of
reality and no way of properly adjudicating between them. However,
Hick claimed to be a realist and, moreover, he held a strong view in
the goodness of ultimate reality and in our obligation as humans to
conform to that goodness. He was an optimist who looked beyond this
life to the reality of an eternal life. These are metaphysical beliefs. Yet
critical realism, when pushed to the extremes, can break any connection
with reality. An "object" of belief can eventually drop out as irrelevant.

The existence of different religions poses a problem with which Hick
tries to come to grips. Are we to be exclusivists, saying only our own
religion is right? Are we to recognize that many religions overlap in their
beliefs and even, as, say, in the case of Christianity and Judaism, share
much content? In that case, we may want to be inclusivist, recognizing
the good and truth that lies in other religions. We are, though, still

---

28 Hick, *An Interpretation of Religion*, p. 247.

judging everything in terms of our beliefs. Might we recognize, however, that at times we can learn from other religions? Then we begin to tread the path to a pluralism that can result in us upholding the equality of all religions. That brings us to the brink of relativism, as we run the risk of losing all contact with any idea of truth.

In its pursuit of an equality between all "great" religions, Hick's revisionist approach to doctrine raises questions about the status of what we are doing. Philosophy of religion ought to be a neutral discipline, describing what is at stake in different understandings of religion. Once it gets launched into particular doctrinal disputes within a religion, about, say, the Virgin Birth or the Incarnation, it can become a very different animal, even indulging in advocacy for radical forms of Christian theology. Wittgensteinians found themselves in a similar predicament when their "neutral" description of the character of religious belief came to be rejected vehemently by many believers.

Hick's philosophy of religion brings the same type of problem. A philosopher is telling believers what their beliefs amount to, even if they vehemently reject the claim. If Hick is right about the relation of religious belief to the Real, traditional Christian believers are just mistaken. They merely exhibit one cultural "manifestation" of the Real (whatever that manifestation's precise connection with it may be). Hick's hope is that this will induce humility in religion and a willingness to learn from others. Yet all knowledge seems to be placed beyond our reach. Unless others know more than we do, there seems to be nothing to learn.

Relativism and its fellow travelers are marketed as promoting tolerance, but any intellectual motive for mutual understanding has been largely removed. If all beliefs are equally distant from the truth, why do we need to engage in dialogue with those who think differently? They know no more than we do and are merely reflecting their cultures. Yet there is an even more corrosive element to this thought: Why should one even go on holding on to one's own beliefs? A Christian who believes that God was uniquely revealed through Jesus Christ might come to think that there is little point in the Christian worship reflecting that belief if it is only a cultural construct. The silence of a Quaker meeting might appear to be an attractive alternative if one even wants to continue with any corporate activity.

Hick is motivated by the need to encourage "dialogue" between religion, but it is unclear what the basis might be for that. Ratzinger points out the way dialogue has acquired a relativist meaning. He says that dialogue "has become the very epitome of the relativist credo, the concept opposed to that of 'conversion' and mission."[29] Ratzinger sees dialogue as "an exchange between positions that are fundamentally of equal status and thus mutually relative." Yet full-blooded relativism carries with it greater dangers. Dialogue itself requires some shared basis – namely, the objective reality we all confront and a shared human nature. If Hick's views are pushed to their logical conclusion, dialogue becomes impossible.

We must not assume that divine reality is totally beyond our reach if we are to compare different understandings of it. The blind men were actually in contact with an elephant, and we can refer to their different perceptions of the same object. There is some commonality. As a result, the perceptions have to cohere, since they are partial glimpses of the same reality. If one of them had reported the experience of floating in water or of touching what were, in fact, blades of grass waving in the wind, he would not have been talking about the elephant at all. To enter into any dialogue, we all have to be situated in the same reality, even if some of our beliefs diverge. Otherwise, we will be forever talking past each other. Dialogue has to be an anti-relativist concept. Even the idea that different religions are of equal status is a sophisticated one, and it requires some criterion to judge their equality. Learning from each other only makes sense when we are all trying to understand one world.

---

29 Ratzinger, *Truth and Tolerance*, p. 120.

4

THE ROOTS OF
RELIGIOUS BELIEF

CAN GOD BE KNOWN?

God, or Ultimate Reality, may be beyond our full comprehension, but such a reality, if it exists, cannot be completely hidden from us unless it is to be ignored. The tradition in Christian theology of the so-called *via negativa* sees God as so wholly "other" that we are aware more of what we cannot say about such a reality than what we can. We know, for instance, that God is no more male than female. That does not mean "He" is a mixture of both, but rather that our human concepts break down when applied to "Him." To refer God as "it" is just as misleading, if, as Christianity wants to affirm, "He" is personal, and humans can enter into a relationship with "Him." They can refer to Him as "Our Father," but realize that in any human sense He is not our father at all. Language breaks down at this point, but is the alternative (as some have argued) total silence?

The further Hick pushed the idea of "The Real" away from its grounding in any particular religion, the easier it was for it to lose all meaning, or to convey a misleading one. A nothing would serve as well as a something about which nothing could be said. Any realist understanding, we must stress again, has to accept that objective reality may exist in its own right and be independent of all human knowledge. Yet God's existence is not just a matter of fact, however interesting, about the furniture of the universe. God, if He exists and has created us, must, it is supposed by different religions, be related to us in some way. His is not the reality posited by deists who, particularly in the eighteenth century, saw God as the Being who had wound up the clock-work of the universe and then lost all interest in its development; who proclaimed the laws of nature and then immediately retired. A God of love could never be like that, but must be in some kind of relationship with those who, it is alleged, were created in His image.

This picture demands an understanding of the God with whom we are supposed to relate. If He (for want of a better pronoun) is totally "other" so that we can only say what He is not, and cannot even use personal language and pronouns to refer to Him, the gap between Creator and creatures widens so as to be unbridgeable. Many would want to invoke the language of mystery, which indicates that there are undeniable limits to our understanding. If we could fully understand God and His nature, we would become God. Going to the other extreme is just as dangerous, and we are then back facing Wittgenstein's warning about the functioning of concepts. A God that we know nothing about, and cannot conceive of at all, is no different from an absence of God, or no god at all.

The traditional answer to this problem is that of revelation – of a general kind to all humans, or a special one at particular places and times. The idea, for instance, that God is wholly revealed in the person of Jesus brings the unimaginable Godhead down to a level that humans can grasp, because God then speaks, in effect, as a human being to other human beings. Some of Hick's philosophical problems about the inaccessibility of God as a Kantian *noumenon* stemmed from his dismissal of the Incarnation as being a full revelation of God. He wanted to ensure that Christianity was not able to claim any privileged position above other religions. If Christ was truly God, his words would set the standard for all truth. Challenging this, however, had the result of removing Christianity's attempt to answer the question as to how we can know anything about God.

Behind these concerns about the grounding of theistic concepts and the possibility of any human knowledge of the divine, there lurks a major challenge to all religious faith, whether Christian or not. Whatever the doctrines of a particular religion, whether about Old Testament Prophets, the Incarnation, the role of Mohammed and the Qur'an, or whatever else it may be, they may convince the adherents of that religion that in some way they have been given access to some understanding of the nature of the divine. The fact remains that they fail to convince members of other religions. The very plurality of religions may seem to place a question mark over the validity of any.

Why does God make it so difficult for people to come to belief in Him? Even posing this question already tilts the argument in a Christian direction. How do we know in the first place if there are many Gods or one? Polytheism has been rampant throughout human history, even among apparently sophisticated thinkers such as the ancient Greeks and Romans. It has been argued that the idea of monotheism, that of a single principle underlying everything, is both simpler and perhaps more rational than any idea of many competing ones. The scientific quest for a single Theory of Everything is a secular version of the same rational urge that can see one God as the fount of all reason, and of all existence.

Yet the question remains; the gods or God do not seem to make it very easy to believe in them or Him. This is a particularly forceful point if we conceive of one God in personal terms. If we assume that He wishes a relationship with His creatures, as Christianity teaches, that makes it more puzzling why it should be so difficult to believe in Him. Why are there so many competing understandings, and different religious responses, to the nature of whatever Ultimate Reality consists in? The very existence of so many different religions now and throughout history might suggest that, whatever the cause of religious beliefs in humans, they cannot reflect the nature of the reality they claim to describe.

This is linked with issues concerning the objectivity and rationality of religions. Only when a religion attempts to describe and refer to an independently existing reality does it become a problem that there are competing descriptions. It is even more of a problem if, unlike in the physical sciences, there does not appear to be any agreed-on procedure for settling the issue, at least in this life. If, however, religion is dismissed as subjective, it is no longer surprising that different individuals, let alone different cultures, believe different things. The result is that we will learn about them rather than about what actually exists. The stories told in different religions can then be seen as just that, and not vehicles of any kind of truth.

DOES DIVERSITY INDICATE FALSEHOOD?

Instead of just ignoring religion as a matter of subjective test, the very diversity of religious belief can be used as an argument that attempts to expose all of it as based on falsehood. The undoubted existence of many, apparently conflicting, religious beliefs can itself be used as an argument to undermine all religion. Instead of accepting religious faith as a personal quirk of some, perhaps to be respected, such faith can be made to look simply mistaken. It is easy to move from the view that religious belief is not a matter of reason to the view that it is positively irrational and should be repudiated. Let us take a belief in one personal God, as is posited by Christianity. If there is such a God, we would expect Him to try to form a personal relationship with all humans. Yet the fact of religious diversity makes it all too likely, it could be argued, that our beliefs and ability to come to any knowledge of such a God will depend on cultural factors. It is a matter of pure chance. We have already encountered this long-standing argument. In the nineteenth century, John Stuart Mill used it when writing "On Liberty." He suggested that people were influenced by the cultural context and were able to ignore the fact that different societies, building different worlds, came to radically different beliefs. He says of "a man":

He devolves upon his own world the responsibility of being in the right against the dissentient worlds of other people; and it never troubles him that mere accident has decided which of these numerous worlds is the object of his reliance, and that the same causes which make him a Churchman in London, would have made him a Buddhist or a Confucian in Pekin.[1]

This presupposes a more widespread agreement and sharing of assumptions than is likely to exist in any given society today. The issue has become not just the beliefs of a whole society against those of another society. It is now by no means certain that a Londoner would be a "Churchman." Nevertheless, the fact of diversity suggests it is a matter of chance that one grew up in one country or home, with one set of beliefs, rather than in another, with a different set. Whether relativism (about the beliefs of a supposedly monolithic society) descends to subjectivism (about the reactions of individuals) or not, both are united in denying the idea of an independently existing reality to which some respond in a religious way and some do not. Both say that religious belief is haphazard and accidental. The extreme variation we encounter across places and times looks like an argument for that

1 J. S. Mill *On Liberty, Utilitarianism*, ed. Mary Warnock, Fontana, London, 1962 p. 144.

position. Once one turns to it, and encounters persistent and profound religious disagreement, it is tempting to dismiss the validity of all such belief.

On one hand, if reference to the transcendent appears redundant, religious diversity is only to be expected, with no constraints on the side of an objective reality to regulate our belief. On the other hand, if a personal God were understood as trying to be revealed to us, radical religious disagreement, and a bewildering variety of religious experiences, should be surprising. Otherwise, many other factors may well be at work directing our beliefs. Those would vary from society to society, and from social context to social context. The radical diversity of religions and other worldviews is, it would be argued, only to be expected from what we might term a "naturalistic" point of view, seeing everything in terms that science can explain, at least in principle.

Varying social backgrounds may ensure that any human propensity to religious belief is expressed in different ways. We dress differently in different societies, eat different food, speak different languages, and so on, even if these characteristics are no doubt all impelled by the basic demands and features of human nature. Different environments will produce different responses. The same urges will be at work underlying religious practices, and, the story goes, once they have been identified, the next step will be to explain their existence by an appeal to their adaptive nature. They will be connected with what has proved beneficial from an evolutionary point of view. Arguments rage as to whether religion has been built into our nature or is itself a by-product, presumably accidental, of other characteristics that have been built into human nature for other reasons. A complication is that even though religious dispositions could have arisen because they are riding on the back of other characteristics, their persistence in human societies may well rest on the fact that religion has proved beneficial. It might, for example, encourage altruism, even self-sacrifice, and that may help a society flourish in ways that would not occur of there was a "war of all against all."

In its early days in the late 1970s, sociobiology tried to explain morality in terms of "kin selection" (favoring relatives, particularly children) and "reciprocal altruism" (helping you in expectation that the favor would be returned.)[2] Now, however, there is a greater realization among many scientists that so-called group selection may be at work. In other words, groups can create the conditions in which individuals can flourish and pass on their genes more successfully. "Individual selection" based on the competition for reproductive success between individuals may not tell the whole story. This is important because it builds a place for religion, explaining its persistence and importance in all societies.

It is striking that even the founder of sociobiology, E. O. Wilson, has become more convinced that group selection plays a role in the maintenance of religion in societies. His specific specialty is insect societies, particularly ants, but he has over the years extrapolated from these to form conclusions, often controversial, about the nature of human social interaction. His starting point is that of the philosophical naturalist, trying to explain everything in terms of science. He argues that "there is every good reason to explain the origin of religion and morality as special events in the evolutionary history of humanity driven by natural selection."[3]

Wilson continues by claiming that organized religion is "an expression of tribalism." He says: "Every religion teaches its adherents that they are a special fellowship and that their creation story, moral precepts, and privilege from divine power are superior to those clamed in other religions." He suggests that "their charity and other acts of altruism are concentrated on their coreligionists," and that "the goal of religions is submission to the will and common good of the tribe."[4] Thus it is alleged that competition between "tribes" is the driver for the development of religion.

When tribes are geographically separated and struggling against others for a precarious existence, it is easy to see how this scenario could play out. Loyalty to the tribe, strengthened by religious teaching and precept, could help the whole tribe flourish, even if it involves the self-sacrifice of some. In the process, an environment could be created in

---

2 See Roger Trigg, *The Shaping of Man: Philosophical Aspects of Sociobiology*, Blackwell, Oxford, 1982.
3 E. O. Wilson, *The Social Conquest of the Earth*, Liveright Publishing Corporation, New York, 2012, p. 258.
4 Wilson, *The Social Conquest of the Earth*, p. 258.

which altruism, inspired by religion, could help the common good. Yet by definition, such a restricted view of religion will find it impossible to understand or explain the universal claims of a religion such as Christianity, which typically claims the Christian Gospel is intended "for all." Wilson grudgingly admits that altruism could be extended to outsiders but this "is usually to proselytize and thereby strengthen the size of the tribe."[5] Yet this remark reveals how fuzzy his idea of a tribe is. He seems to have shifted from a conventional idea of a tribe living together to that of the scattered adherents of a religion, who may themselves belong to very different societies and nationalities. His view of religion can hardly make sense of any religion that claims to be speaking to all humans and is universalist in its approach.

THE COGNITIVE SCIENCE OF RELIGION

Naturalist accounts of religion, in fact, face a difficulty in that they themselves want to make universal claims about religion, based on common features of humanity. They typically make generalizations about human nature. Yet they have to recognize that these may interact with local conditions to produce many different kinds of beliefs and practices. They are, therefore, stronger in dealing with the general features of human minds that recur across cultures than explaining why these may differ in the way they are expressed in different cultures. That indeed is not their job. An example of this is the so-called cognitive science of religion, a relatively new discipline that draws on cognitive science to explain the mental tools used in helping build a religious vision of the world.

An array of different mental tendencies and intuitions common to humanity come into play. We all, it appears, find it easy to look for purpose in the world. The psychologist Dorothy Kelemen has conducted many studies that show how children, and even adults, naturally see that a biological and physical world was made by an agent for a purpose. There is what she terms a "human predilection for intentional explanation."[6] This links with the "mental tool" to which psychologists have given the acronym HADD: hypersensitive agent detection

---

5 Wilson, *The Social Conquest of the Earth*, p. 259.
6 Dorothy Kelemen, "Are Children 'Intuitive Theists'? Reasoning about Purpose and Design in Nature." *Psychological Science*, 2004, 15, p. 296.

device. We naturally expect agency in the natural world. We all know how easy it is to jump at the rustle of leaves in a dark wood, or a loud noise upstairs in an apparently empty house. It is natural to wonder who or what is there and to assume that the noise has been produced by an agent. The psychologist Justin Barrett refers to HADD as a crude and non-reflective system for detecting agency. As he says, "If you bet that something is an agent and it isn't, not much is lost. But if you bet that something is not an agent and it turns out to be one, you could be lunch."[7] What has this got to do with religion, or with notions of the transcendent? The theory would be that a tendency to look for agency can result in unseen agents being posited, when there are no obvious agents. Angels, spirits, and demons are but some of the alleged beings that can be invoked. Indeed, much ancient religion revolved round the attribution of personal agency for physical events that could not be easily explained in a nonscientific age. Thunderbolts were the work of Zeus, the force of the sea under the control of Poseidon, and so on. Science has progressed through finding physical explanations for what was previously seen as the work of mysterious agents of this kind.

We are not born, it appears, with fully developed notions of God, but neither is our mind a blank slate on which experience writes. We are not passive observers of the world; our cognitive equipment alerts us to what is salient in the environment. The very nature of human beings is constituted by the way we react to our environment. Human nature does matter. Human cognitive equipment, comprising mental tools, may not always operate on a conscious level, but it enables us to treat some features of our environment as more relevant than others. Our experience is already colored by particular tendencies and constraints. We find it easier to think in some ways than in others.

This particularly matters in the sphere of religion. One way of putting it is to say that humans are naturally religious. This might seem an outrageous statement in an age when atheism seems to be gaining ground in many Western countries. Yet the allegation, particularly from proponents of the cognitive science of religion, is that atheism is a more sophisticated position than are ordinary religious responses to the world. It is to be seen on a level with reasoned theological discourses that themselves attempt to make sense of such responses. Indeed, one writer has

7 J. Barrett, *Why Would Anyone Believe in God?*, p. 31ff.

gone further and argued that "religion is cognitively natural and that science is not."[8] His point is that science produces radically counterintuitive ideas (such as that tables are not solid but composed of electrons), whereas we find it much easier to think in terms that are conducive to religion. He steers clear of saying that certain concepts are innate, but concentrates on the fact, as he sees it, that certain operations are what he terms "maturationally natural."[9] In other words, we develop so as to have them, just as we naturally learn to walk even though we are not born with the ability to walk. He defines such operations, cognitive, perceptual, and motor, as "those that are effortless, automatic, unreflective" and indeed mostly unconscious.[10] He says later that for "human minds deepest maturationally natural dispositions are profoundly difficult either to shake or correct." They are entrenched in us. It would be profoundly significant if they were such as to incline us, as humans, to religion. Indeed, his claim is that possessing such capacities and concepts "equips people, including children, to acquire religion in a way that is not at all true of science."[11]

This last claim is not as outrageous as it might initially appear to some. First, it by no means says anything about the truth or the reliability of the beliefs of either. It merely points out the comparative difficulty human minds have in grasping each. Second, it does justice to the undoubted fact of the universality or near-universality of religion in human history. All societies, it is often claimed, have contained religious beliefs, usually in a very prominent way. It is a sad fact that very few societies in the course of human history have gained much scientific knowledge. The advanced societies of our contemporary world are the exception, not the rule. As a result McCauley can claim with some plausibility (and with no implications as to what is true) that "on this account of human cognitive development, it is atheism, not religion, that humans must work to apply."[12]

We have already mentioned our human tendency to detect agency and purpose in the world. Others have picked out the fact we are, in a

---

8 Robert N. McCauley, *Why Religion Is Natural and Science Is Not*, Oxford University Press, New York, 2011, p. 3.
9 McCauley, *Why Religion Is Natural and Science Is Not*, p. 59.
10 McCauley, *Why Religion Is Natural and Science Is Not*, p. 59.
11 McCauley, *Why Religion Is Natural and Science Is Not*, p. 119.
12 McCauley, *Why Religion Is Natural and Science Is Not*, p. 221.

way, "natural dualists," in that we seem to find it easy to conceive of mind and body as separate. Anthropologists have found a fundamental cognitive tendency, as one puts it, "to view ourselves and others as immaterial minds or souls, occupying bodies."[13] This is the edge of a vast philosophical controversy, and goes against many of the assumptions of modern science. Appeals to the merits and demerits of such dualism involve very sophisticated philosophical positions. The point here is that our starting point as ordinary human beings means that we find it remarkably easy to conceive of mind apart from body. As Paul Bloom says, "We are natural Cartesians – dualistic thinking comes naturally to us."[14] We are very ready to conceive of survival in some way after the death of the body. This again is not an argument establishing truth, but rather concerns what we as humans find easy to understand. If you recount a near-death experience, of the kind that is well documented, of apparently looking down on your body in a hospital when you were unconscious and even at the point of death, whatever our rational reaction, we have no difficulty understanding what you are describing. It is all too easy to imagine. The dualist presupposition, whether well grounded or not, that I am not my body takes over.

This is connected with what psychologists have called Theory of Mind, which enables people to attribute mental properties to other agents. It does not seem to be completely established in children until about age four, when they are able to see how things are from the perspective of someone else. In the end, I not only have to understand what you are thinking, and whether it differs from what I am thinking. I also have to come to be able to understand what you think about what I am thinking. An interesting experiment, of a kind reported, for instance, by Justin Barrett, but often referred to, and repeated, shows how children at the age of three assume that their mother knows everything they know.[15] By age four they understand that they may not have seen what they have seen. Suppose you put an apple under one of two cups, in front of a child, when a child's mother sees what you are doing. You then move it under the other cup after she has left the

---

13 Emma Cohen, *The Mind Possessed: The Cognition of Spirit Possession in an Afro-Brazilian Religious Tradition*, Oxford University Press, Oxford, 2005, p. 1402.
14 Paul Bloom, *Descartes' Baby*, Arrow Books, London 2005, p. xii.
15 Barrett, *Why Would Anyone Believe in God?*, pp. 56–57.

room. The child at age three will be sure that mummy will know where the apple now is when she comes back. At age four they realize she will not.

An interesting extension of this experiment, also described by Barrett, shows that children are quite ready to go on saying, when asked, that God will know what has happened to the apple. God is not restricted, but has an infallibility, even omniscience, that the child's mother is no longer seen as having. Children are ready to accept that God knows everything. A common response to this is that it merely shows something about a child's background and what a child has been taught. There may be something in that, although the results tend to apply across cultures. Even so, the response misses the point, which is not what children actually believe, but what they find easy to understand. At age three they think that mummy knows whatever they do. They soon come to learn that this not the case. Even so, they find it quite easy, even natural, to continue to imagine that God has different capacities from humans, and to understand what these capacities are. Far from "omniscience" being a complicated philosophical notion arrived at by extrapolating from human experience to an unimaginable degree, something quite like it seems to inhere in our earliest childish ideas about what others, particularly our parents, can understand. Understanding it seems to be one of earliest mental tools.

Barrett's own conclusion is that "we find thinking about God as superknowing or infallible rather easy."[16] A postscript to this is that this belief can be salutary and important in the enforcement of morality, and hence for the flourishing of a society. Cheating and deception may be deterred if people think they are always within the sight of God, just as the presence of closed-circuit television cameras in a modern city can deter criminal behavior. That might, from an evolutionary point of view, reinforce the impact of religion on a given society and, given forms of group selection, ensure its persistence. This will particularly be the case if God is regarded as "good," possessing the moral character of, say, the author of the Ten Commandments.

The cognitive science of religion is often coupled with such evolutionary reasoning, but it is important to see that its claims about how

---

16 Barrett, *Why Would Anyone Believe in God?*, p. 80.

humans think across cultures depend on empirical findings, not on evolutionary theory. How people think and why those patterns of thought become established in our cognitive architecture are two distinct questions. What inclines us to religious understandings of the world? Those with a naturalistic view of the world, depending on science, will rule out by definition the idea that these religious impulses could be directed at anything real beyond the physical world. Yet any scientific account of the development of religion sees more similarity than difference at the root of all religion. Even assuming that many conceptual and cognitive capacities join together in helping form what is loosely called a religious view, their repertoire is not unlimited. Robert McCauley stresses that "the mind does not contain a specific 'department' of religion." He continues: "Humans' religious predilections are understood as by-products of our natural cognitive capacities."[17] This suggests that this is all the accidental, chance result of the evolutionary development of other capacities, and there is room for debate about that. The crucial point, however, is that characteristically religious dispositions are intimately bound up with the very idea of what it is to think as a human being.

IS RELIGIOUS DIVERSITY SUPERFICIAL?

Religion, or rather the various impulses that give rise to religion, has deep roots in human nature. All the religions of the world, in all their apparent diversity, can be traced to the same origin. Why, then, do similar foundations have such different edifices built on them? McCauley deals with this and claims that, in contrast to science, which flourishes with original ideas, religion does not trade in novelty. Religion rests on what he terms "a small number of variations on a limited set of elements." He says:

The superficial diversity notwithstanding, religions hare the same cognitive origins and vary within the same limited framework of natural cognitive constraints. Science overturns those constraints and regularly produces new, original ideas. Religion mainly obeys those constraints and replays minor variations on the same ideas time and time again.[18]

17 McCauley, *Why Religion Is Natural and Science Is Not*, p. 154.
18 McCauley, *Why Religion Is Natural and Science Is Not*, p. 152.

The naturalist may feel that all that is necessary in a scientific approach to religion is to uncover the cognitive mechanisms that build religious pictures of the world. These are seen as concerned with agency detection, Theory of Mind, beliefs in life after death, dispositions to see purpose, and so on. Suggesting that they are mere by-products of more essential parts of human cognitive functioning would seem to have explained away religion. Yet naturalism cannot of itself explain diversity. It traffics in universal similarities and must leave the undoubted differences to the social anthropologist and others to explain. Its temptation is to underplay the significance of religious diversity. Explanation of "religion" in terms of evolved capacities seems enough to offer a scientific account of its origin and persistence. "Religion" becomes an all-inclusive concept, and differences between religions become of little account.

All this was particularly apparent in one of E. O. Wilson's earliest attempts to see religion in terms of biology. In his seminal *On Human Nature*,[19] which in 1978 was a foundation document of sociobiology, he prefigures the themes of his advocacy of group selection in attempting to give a scientific explanation of religion. He says: "The final decisive edge enjoyed by scientific naturalism will come from its capacity to explain traditional religion, its chief competitor, as a wholly material phenomenon."[20] He has to discount all references to the transcendent as so much froth, which do not drive the belief. Yet for religious believers of all kinds, the content of their beliefs cannot be dismissed in this way because it constitutes what the belief is. They could never accept that their beliefs were fundamentally the same as those of every other religion.

For Wilson – and, one suspects, many scientists – "religion" is an all-purpose category into which many disparate beliefs are bundled so that religion can be given an explanation. Given some explanation about why religious beliefs are held, details about differences between them can be ignored. Wilson claimed from the beginning that religion confers biological advantage. He says: "When the gods are served, the Darwinian fitness of the members of the tribe is the ultimate if recognised beneficiary." He elaborates this by saying that "the blinding force

19 E. O. Wilson, *On Human Nature*, Harvard University Press, Cambridge, MA, 1978.
20 Wilson, *On Human Nature*, p. 192.

of religious allegiance can operate in the absence of theology." In illustration, he continues: "The May Day rallies of T'ien An Men Square would have been instantly understood by the Mayan multitudes, Lenin's tomb by the worshippers of Christ's bloodied shroud."[21]

When a functional account of religion is produced, saying, for instance, that it increases biological fitness, any religion may qualify. Moreover, any other belief system or practice that fulfills the same function will be swept up into the general category of religion so that the category itself becomes meaningless. The differences between religions are ignored, and the distinction between religion and other worldviews is also flattened out, so that a system of state atheism itself qualifies as being as religious as the religion it is trying to replace.

Even when we introduce the more nuanced view of religion encouraged by the cognitive science of religion, the distinctiveness of religious concepts may be stressed, but they are still bound up in more general cognitive mechanisms. That means that universal features of human understanding are picked out to the detriment of the features of particular beliefs. Yet those particular beliefs are the lifeblood of each religion. Science may explain a disposition to believe in divine agency, but not the belief that God, or gods, have acted in particular ways, or why *this* rather than *that* belief is adopted. Perhaps the content of belief does not matter. We are just predisposed to have beliefs of a particular kind, and the form they take is irrelevant as long as they are all performing the same function. The tough-minded scientific naturalist may say that, but it will be far from the case for the religious believer.

Wilson, and others, may say that we pick up whatever beliefs our tribes have, but this seems implausible in a pluralistic society with many beliefs competing against one another. What counts as our respective "tribe"? There is danger of circularity here. Our tribe is the group that holds a belief in *x*. We believe in *x* because we belong to that tribe. This ignores the fact that beliefs are held because they are held to be true. Practices and rituals depend on certain views of the world and our place as humans in it, and such views can diverge dramatically. Diversity is not just a matter of superficial variation of an underlying similarity. The differences between religions will always go much deeper than that.

---

21 Wilson, *On Human Nature*, p. 184.

THE SIGNIFICANCE OF DIFFERENT BELIEFS

The cognitive science of religion, backed up by evolutionary accounts of religion, demonstrates that religion is deeply rooted in human nature. Even atheists may find themselves thinking in ways that lead to religion, even if their reason inclines them to dismiss such reactions as infantile. There may be a general preparedness for religion in the human mind, and a receptivity for certain ways of understanding our surroundings. There is still a question about the content of those understandings. We may well be inclined to accept the possibility of spiritual or divine agency, but that cannot tell us the form we believe it will take. Are we going to think that Zeus has caused the thunder, or that there is one God who has created the world in a rational manner that grounds the scientific explanation of lightning and thunder? We may not even need the wider theological framework of a religion to react in particular ways. We could find it easy to imagine the existence of ghosts and poltergeists, independently of the doctrines of any religion.

The cognitive science of religion appears to explain every kind of belief. It can explain animism and polytheism as easily as monotheism. Yet religion is not like that for a believer. No believer, unless under the influence of a philosophical theory, would say that any form of religious belief is as good as any other. As we have seen, even a belief that different religions can possess distinct, but equally valid, revelations is itself a particular belief ruling out less tolerant alternatives. For participants, the content of belief matters. Changing from one religion to another is possible, just as one can go from belief to unbelief, or the other way round. Doing so, however, is usually a major step involving even a change in way of life, as well as the way one interprets the world. Religious diversity is not superficial, as McCauley claimed. It may develop from a prepared basis in human nature. The different superstructures built on the same foundations are each of very great significance.

One of the most influential philosophers of religion at the end of the twentieth and the beginning of the twenty-first first century was Alvin Plantinga. He took up the idea of what the Protestant reformer, John Calvin, called the sense of divinity (*sensus divinitatis*). Plantinga explains this as "a disposition or set of dispositions to form theistic beliefs in various circumstances, in response to the sorts of conditions or stimuli that trigger the working of this sense of divinity."[22] As he notes, Calvin was impressed by nature's spectacles, and in particular by the wonder evoked by looking at the starry heavens. It is intriguing that Plantinga stresses that knowledge of God need not be innate, but that the capacity for developing it may be. In this he is invoking the idea of "maturationally natural" skills, described earlier in the chapter. The beliefs we come to in this way provide us with a starting point for thought. In Plantinga's terminology, they are "basic in the sense that the beliefs in question are not accepted on the evidential basis of other beliefs." In that sense they are on a par, Plantinga claims, with "perception, memory, and *a priori* belief."[23] They do not always convey knowledge and can be corrected, but the idea is that our minds have a bias toward divinity.

Plantinga sees the sense of divinity as being like other belief-producing faculties or mechanisms. The cognitive science of religion appears to end up with a very similar picture. Both positions – one from the standpoint of science, and the other from that of philosophy and Christian theology – see our thought of the divine as stemming from a natural faculty common to all humans. It produces in us inclinations, or dispositions, to hold certain types of beliefs. It remains to be seen how trustworthy they are. One difficulty is that both Calvin and Plantinga jump quickly from the notion of divinity to that of God. Plantinga quotes Calvin as saying that the conviction that there is "some God" is born naturally in us all.[24] Plantinga sees the heavens as proclaiming "the glory of God."[25] Indeed, his path from divinity to "some God" and then to the Christian God seems to be very short. There may be reason to write in this way from the standpoint of Christian theology, but it begs the important question of how specific the deliverances of our cognitive mechanisms can be. A predisposition to religious belief appears to support the existence, both now and in the past, of myriad forms of religion, and does not seem to support a fully formed belief in the one Creator God of Christian belief. That is to make too big a jump. Calvin's vague reference to divinity was more accurate. Whether

22 Alvin Plantinga, *Warranted Christian Belief*, Oxford University Press, New York, 2000, p. 179.
23 Plantinga, *Warranted Christian Belief*, p. 175.
24 Plantinga, *Warranted Christian Belief*, p. 172.
25 Plantinga, *Warranted Christian Belief*, p. 175.

everyone is presented with a *sensus Dei*, a sense of the presence of one God, seems much more questionable.

Religion may be fundamental in human understanding, and not easily eradicated. Plantinga himself suggests that "awareness of God is natural, widespread, and not easy to forget."[26] As he points out, the persistence of religion in Eastern Europe and in the former Soviet Union, despite fierce attempts under communism to stamp it out, bear out this claim. Yet the reference to God fails to take proper account of the fact of religious diversity. The mechanisms described by the cognitive science of religion may underpin all religious beliefs, but because those can be of so many different kinds, the mechanisms certainly underdetermine them. Other factors have to come into play to explain the mere fact of such radical difference.

We asked earlier why God was so hidden from us if there was a loving God who wished to be in relation with us. Religious diversity suggests that there is no clear path to religious belief of the kind we might hope for if there was a God. Yet the human mind has an initial bias toward the divine. We find it easy to have ideas about divinity so that, after all, it does not appear totally incomprehensible. The idea of the transcendent and supernatural beyond the physical world is not so strange or hard to grasp. For good or ill, human minds are prepared for religious belief.

26 Plantinga, *Warranted Christian Belief*, p. 173.

5

DOES DISAGREEMENT
UNDERMINE THEISM?

Some theologians and philosophers pass too quickly from a *sensus divinitatis* to the idea of the Christian God. Alternatively, some of those dealing with the cognitive science of religion are so ready to turn to a naturalistic explanation of all religion that they are willing to lump everything in the one category. In both cases, the challenge of religious diversity can be quickly passed over. Theologians can ignore it by simply concentrating on the tenets of one religion. In the case of naturalism, an apparent scientific explanation may explain "religion" but goes nowhere in explaining "diversity."

From a theological point of view, some see diversity as a greater obstacle to faith than the existence of evil in the world. If it seems difficult to imagine that a good God could allow so much human suffering, by the same token, why would a caring God be ready to leave so many humans in ignorance of His nature? The atheist can easily say that when there are so many competing beliefs about what is true of the gods, God, or whatever, there is no principled reason for preferring one over the other. They are all to be accounted equally false, an accidental effect of some external influence. When there is no agreed-on way of deciding between them, as there is in scientific method, why not dismiss them as catchy stories that may appeal to the human mind? The myths about the gods transmitted by Homer can easily, it seems, be put into that category. Why not every other story about God? The cognitive science of religion shows how the human mind can latch on to stories that are "minimally counterintuitive," stories that catch our interest because they are unusual but not excessively so. We can easily remember them, whether they are about talking frogs or beings with supernatural powers.

Against this background, the concept of revelation is important in showing how specific religious knowledge may be obtained. So many conflicting revelations can be claimed, which brings us back to the problem of religious diversity. Even within the historic bounds of Christianity there have been many through the centuries who have wanted to add to the revelation through Christ. Mormons and others have appealed to alleged additional revelations from God. How can they be ruled out, except by begging the question at issue, namely the truth of a particular religious outlook? Even if it is agreed that such accretions are inconsistent with traditional Christianity, why should one alleged revelation be accepted and another not? However, the minute we take all such claims at face value, there is no distinction between, say, St. Paul's conversion on the road to Damascus and a claim that God has spoken to someone to encourage a mass suicide.

This is a problem that exercised the empiricist philosopher John Locke in the seventeenth century. He was a Christian philosopher who wanted to stress that Christianity rested on a rational basis. *The Reasonableness of Christianity* was the title of one of his books. While fully accepting the possibility of revelation, he saw that many claims to divine revelation should not be upheld. He had no room for those (such as, perhaps, early Baptists and Quakers) who followed the subjectivity of an inner light and even judged scripture by it. He talks of those who "feel the hand of God moving them within, and the impulses of the spirit," and therefore think that they cannot be mistaken. As Locke says, "they are sure, because they are sure: and their persuasions are right, only because they are strong in them."[1]

For Locke, the question remains on what grounds something is to be seen as a revelation from God. He says, in a slogan that could describe the purpose behind the whole European Enlightenment, "reason must be our last judge and guide in everything."[2] Yet he is at pains to insist that he does not mean we can reject the idea of divine revelation "by natural principles." Locke fully accepted the role of the supernatural

---

1 John Locke, *Essay Concerning Human Understanding*, edited and abridged by A. S. Pringle-Pattison, Oxford University Press, Oxford, 1924, bk. 4, chap. 19, para. 9, p. 361.
2 Locke, *Essay Concerning Human Understanding*, bk. 4, chap. 19, para 14, p. 362.

but felt that we cannot accept any and every supposed revelation as genuine. Each must be tested. The "internal light of assurance" was not enough;[3] it had to be judged by "reason and the Scripture."[4]

In other words, apparent revelation should cohere with other acknowledged revelation, both belonging to Christianity, in particular, and through human rationality, in general. For Locke, the appeal to reason did not mean sitting in judgment on the very possibility of religion and the supernatural. For him, it was natural revelation "whereby the eternal Father of light, and fountain of all knowledge, communicates to mankind that portion of truth which he has laid within the reach of natural faculties."[5] Locke was a loyal member of the Church of England, and Anglican theology tended to follow this idea that scripture and reason should march together, along with a third component, the tradition of the church.

On this view, human rationality is more than an understanding conditioned by the exigencies of time and place. It is a faculty universally shared by humans across epochs and societies. If one couples this with a stronger view than Locke was willing to accept of faculties that give us a definite bias to various religious beliefs, a commonality of human nature prepares us all to look for religious agents, and our reason gives us all a similar ability to recognize what is true. How does this help with religious diversity? It provides a standard to judge alleged revelation. Locke saw in the English Civil War the damage that could be caused by religious enthusiasts who were sure they were right in their beliefs, even if their opponents had similar grounds for being sure of the opposite. These were all supposedly Christian and guided by the same standards of faith, in particular by the same Bible.

It is difficult enough trying to reconcile different Christians. What standards, then, can be applied to any rational choice between religions? The cognitive science of religion describes predispositions and tendencies. It shows what we can find easily intelligible and ready to grasp. It perhaps provides us with a "God-shaped hole" in our minds that is waiting to be filled. Even that latter description is assuming too much. It remains underdetermined whether we should think of one God

---

3 Locke, *Essay Concerning Human Understanding*, bk. 4, chap. 19, para 15, p. 363.
4 Locke, *Essay Concerning Human Understanding*, Book IV, para 16, p. 363.
5 Locke, *Essay Concerning Human Understanding*, bk. 4, chap. 19, para 15, p. 360.

or of many, or of some other spiritual agency. If Locke, for one, is to be followed, there is a single truth open to all humans and capable of being recognized by them, helped by both general and particular revelation. Yet in the face of competing revelations from different religions, there still seems great difficulty in knowing how to judge between them, without accepting the deliverances of one religion's revelation so as to judge others. Adopting the Christian Bible to judge the Qur'an seems no more principled in the abstract than using the Qur'an to judge the Bible.

There can be no quick knockdown argument to champion the alleged revelation of one religion over that of another. Locke's appeal to our common human rationality, however, should not be dismissed too lightly. Many religious people have come to distrust appeals to reason, and "rationalism" can sometimes even be a synonym for atheism. We have already seen how religion has been made a matter of "faith" rather than reason in contemporary eyes and consigned to the category of the subjective. A firm understanding of the role of reason in religion may prevent this, but only if "reason" is not given the narrow, even antireligious, coloring that the later Enlightenment gave it, particularly in France. For a brief period after the Revolution, churches in France were even converted into so-called Temples of Reason. Reason was defined in terms of a science-based materialism that could have no truck with the supernatural or transcendent. Anything metaphysical was ruled out in ways that were ultimately self-contradictory. The prevailing ideology was itself a metaphysical thesis about the possible composition of reality.

We have already noted the reaction against modernist views of reason in the form of the postmodernist championing of relativism. Reason may not be seen in exclusively materialist terms, but it is then rooted exclusively in different traditions and societies, so that what counts as rational in one will not in another. That protects religion from a frontal attack by those who see science as having monopoly rights to truth, but it situates reason within the traditions of each religion. Yet the same rational principles cannot then be shared by adherents of different religions. It cannot provide a meeting ground for dialogue and the discussion of religious issues. If Locke is right, all humans have a faculty of reasoning that should not be co-opted against religion. His is the voice of the early Enlightenment, extolling reason but seeing it as a God-given gift rather than as an antireligious weapon.

Reason can provide an accessible meeting ground where religious differences can be confronted and discussed. This may seem optimistic, and agreement, or even mutual understanding, will be hard to achieve. Even so, any religion or religious belief that is reluctant to be judged at the bar of unbiased reason implies that it does not really think what it asserts is true. If there is such a thing as objective truth, which is valid for everyone whether they recognize it or not, it should be reasoned about in the hope, if not the confidence, that others too might recognize it. Believers should not be afraid of having their beliefs examined. If they are true, there should always, in fact, be good reasons for accepting them, whether that is recognized or not. If they are false, believers should not go on believing them themselves. That may be what many believers fear, but, if they do, it is an attitude that betrays a lack of confidence in the truth of what they believe. Truth must always be relevant to everyone, even if some will not see it.

EPISTEMIC DISTANCE

As an empiricist, Locke was firmly opposed to the idea of any innate ideas. For him, everything is the result of experience, although we have distinct faculties of mind. Modern science, with an ever-growing knowledge of the human genome, understands that the human mind is not a sponge or a blank slate (a *tabula rasa*) on which experience writes. As cognitive science demonstrates, being human is to have a distinctive cognitive architecture, to have minds set toward particular ways of interpreting the world. Locke, on the other hand, supposes the mind to be "white paper, void of all characters, without any ideas."[6]

The theist might believe that we are not left to the mercy of chance as much as has sometimes been supposed but are already inclined to religious explanations. Even so, we are not naturally led to one religion rather than another, and we are undoubtedly free to reject all religion. It is a fundamental presupposition of much Christian theology that humans have the freedom to choose. Rationality, on this understanding, goes hand in hand with freedom, giving us the capability of making choices for reasons, rather than being compelled.

6 Locke, *Essay Concerning Human Understanding*, bk. 2, chap. 1, para 2, p. 42.

We are not free to determine in any strong sense what is true. We are free, it seems, to make mistakes and misjudgments. Scientists need to be free to test and criticize and probe, no matter where this takes them. Sometimes they will be mistaken, but oppressive, totalitarian regimes do not form a good background for scientific inquiry. In the same way, freedom gives us the responsibility of making our own judgments about religion, even though we may fall into error. Some might think that in an ideal world we would all see what is true for everyone and come to an agreement about it. That, however, removes human freedom. Christian theology would hold that a God who has given us reason, and the freedom with which to exercise it, is not a God who compels faith. The freedom to reject is implied by the very possibility of a free commitment.

John Hick talks of "epistemic distance." He says that this is a "distance in the cognitive dimension." He explains it as a distance, in the case of humans, "in their existence within and as part of a world that functions as an autonomous system and from within which God is not overwhelmingly evident."[7] If, as some theologies do, we regard this world as a vale of soul making we would not expect everything to be blindingly obvious or free from difficulty. Hick refers to this in the context of evil and suffering, but the idea also applies when we are faced with the general difficulty of coming to religious belief. In Christian thinking, the otherness of God, and his transcendence, ensures that our understanding of divine purposes will always be limited. Reference to "mystery" can be a way of not facing awkward questions. The fact remains, however, that if there is a God, whose nature must surpass the knowledge of finite beings, we will always face unanswered questions.

There is a story that Bertrand Russell, the fervently atheist philosopher of the early twentieth century, was asked what he would say if, against all his expectations, he found himself before the throne of God after his death. He said he would ask, "Why didn't you give more evidence of your existence?" This is a common feeling, particularly, perhaps, among the more philosophically inclined. Yet anything short of absolutely convincing evidence might still not be enough, and such evidence would compel belief and remove our freedom.

---

7 John Hick, "An Iranaean Theodicy," in *Encountering Evil*, ed. Stephen T. Davis, Westminster John Knox Press, Louisville, KY, 2001, p. 42.

Religious diversity may give more scope for exercising human freedom and be a consequence of that freedom. It is not a new problem. Old Testament prophets were forever inveighing against the backsliding of the Jews toward indigenous religions. The prophets of Baal were only one group of many competitors through the centuries. The books of the New Testament were written amid the utmost religious diversity. Mohammed lived in a religiously diverse world and was very conscious of how the "religions of the book," Judaism and Christianity, were practiced. No major religion, including all the presently existing "world religions," has had a clear run, without having to displace predecessors and compete with rivals. Sometimes the process took a physical form, as when Christian churches were built on the site of Roman temples.

This means that the idea that religious diversity creates any new challenge not previously encountered is implausible. Robert McKim argues that "it is difficult for the major religions to treat each other with adequate seriousness."[8] He continues, "Yet the traditions will increasingly have to confront the significance of diversity. There is no escaping the fact that the presence of competing traditions confronts each of the traditions in a new and more forceful way."[9] There are two issues here, each of which is important. The first is the philosophical question of the significance of the existence of varying and competing religions, all of which cannot be equally true. The other question, to which we shall return, is the more political issue of how, given recent movements of population, different religions can properly coexist alongside each other. By running the two together, the intellectual problem is made to seem new. However, what is new may be the way in which different parts of the world, and different religions, are now, under so-called globalization, made more aware of each other.

DOUBT AND COMMITMENT

Human freedom means that there is room for honest doubt as well as full-hearted commitment. An ongoing problem is how far such doubt should undermine the full commitment that different religions seem to demand. Religious diversity can, it seems, be itself a reason for hesitancy

8 Robert McKim, *On Religious Diversity*, Oxford University Press, New York, 2012, p. 3.
9 McKim, *On Religious Diversity*, p. 4.

and tentative belief. McKim brings this out very forcefully when he asks the perennial question of why it is not more obvious that God exists.[10] He continues, "And do the competing claims of the traditions cancel each other out as far as their believability is concerned?" His own conclusion is that "God's hiddenness creates uncertainty, and contributes to profound disagreement about the existence and nature of God."[11]

He is one of those who suggest that it contributes more to unbelief than does the venerable problem of evil. It is certainly easier to take beliefs for granted in a settled society, in which a certain type of religious belief is so built into its foundations that it becomes part of the identity of the citizens. In a pluralistic society, containing competing beliefs and the challenge of total unbelief, things become more confused. That is the position in contemporary Western societies. But as was seen in, say, New Testament times, the presence of competitors does not have to lessen the belief of some in one particular religion.

McKim believes that the existence of disagreement in religious matters must lessen confidence in the truth of any particular religious belief. He says, "Given the extent of the disagreement on religious matters, the confidence with which people make pronouncements on matters of religious importance, and the conviction with which the relevant beliefs are held, are remarkable."[12] He thinks that certainty, or even some confidence about the truth of anything, should be eroded by the existence of disagreement. One only has to apply this rule to nonreligious matters to see that it is implausible. A scientist who has rigorously tested a theory in a new area, and produced controversial results that do not find ready acceptance by colleagues, may persevere and indeed, through a commitment to what is being proposed, may one day succeed in getting it established as accepted science. Yet that would only happen because of an initial willingness not to give in to conventional opinion.

In less abstruse areas, nothing is so obvious that someone may not disbelieve it. People can be irrational, stupid, or willfully stubborn. They are reluctant to accept new ideas. Some, even today, may still insist that the earth is flat, producing elaborate conspiracy theories as to why

---

10 Robert McKim, *Religious Ambiguity and Religious Diversity*, Oxford University Press, New York, 2001, p. xi.
11 McKim, *Religious Ambiguity and Religious Diversity*, p. 12.
12 McKim, *Religious Ambiguity and Religious Diversity*, p. 129.

photographs from space are forgeries. That should not lessen our own certainty that the earth is round. Even basic mathematical truths can be contradicted, particularly when they get more complicated than two plus two equals four. This should not undermine our own confidence in their truth.

This is far from saying that those who contradict each other in the sphere of religion are necessarily stupid or irrational. The fact that God, if there is one, may be partially hidden from us has to leave room for different notions of the divine. Given less than complete information, people will inevitably draw different conclusions. As has been pointed out in the philosophy of science, theories can be underdetermined by the relevant data, and different theories can be empirically equivalent.[13] They rest on the same empirical base but still make different assertions about the nature of the world. This is particularly the case in fields such as cosmology, in which knowledge may at best be partial. A favorite everyday example of the American philosopher W. V. Quine was the interpretation of a series of sinuous shapes appearing and disappearing in a line in the water. Is it one Loch Ness Monster or several smaller creatures, such as dolphins, leaping in and out of the water in unison? A glimpse may not suffice to determine the matter, and the animal or animals may then disappear. The data we have could support either interpretation. So it can be with more complicated scientific theories, and so, it might be alleged, it is with ideas of divinity.

Does this mean that we should be detached about the alleged truth of such underdetermined issues? Parallels with scientific knowledge might reinforce this view. A scientist must be ready to criticize a theory and even to give it up in the face of countervailing empirical evidence. Some, such as Karl Popper, have argued that the correct scientific attitude is not only to be constantly questioning theories and trying to probe their weaknesses but, as a consequence, to hold them only tentatively. He upholds "the critical attitude," as opposed to the dogmatic handing on of a tradition.[14] All science is then provisional, and scientific progress is only possible if scientists recognize that and are willing to change their

---

13 For a discussion of W. V. Quine's view of science, see, for instance, Roger Trigg, *Reality at Risk: A Defence of Realism in Philosophy and the Sciences*, 2nd ed., Hemel, Hempstead, 1989, p. 67.
14 See, for example, Karl Popper, *Objective Knowledge*, Oxford University Press, Oxford, 1972, p. 347.

minds. According to this view, agnosticism about the truth of scientific theories is built into the nature of scientific method. However, transferring that approach to the realm of religion would make agnosticism the only rational outcome.

Richard Dawkins, the atheist biologist, talks of his belief in the truths of evolution and their fascination and beauty. He writes, "My belief in evolution is not fundamentalism, and it is not faith, because I know what it would take to change my mind, and I would gladly do so if the necessary evidence were forthcoming."[15] We have here an intended contrast between the alleged irrationality of a "fundamentalist" faith and the rationality of science. For Dawkins, "fundamentalists know that they are right because they have read the truth in a holy book and they know, in advance, that nothing will budge them from their belief."[16] Yet Dawkins is happy to use the word "passion" in describing his belief in evolution, admitting that he may well, as he puts it, "appear passionate when I defend evolution against a fundamentalist creationist."[17] He claims that he can separate the commitment he brings to his belief in evolution and his advocacy of it with the status of the belief itself.

Dawkins does not let the persistent opposition of creationists, or indeed their existence, to shake his commitment while claiming that he could be shaken from his belief by good scientific evidence, which he does not believe will be forthcoming. Furious disagreement stemming from large sections of some societies, and indeed reflecting long-held views, does not appear to Dawkins to be relevant to the issue of the truth of evolution. He is backing his own scientific expertise, and claim to knowledge, against what he sees as culpable unwillingness to face facts.

Some could dismiss this approach by Dawkins as another version of a dogmatic assertion of truth that is as little based on reason as his opponents'. He certainly narrows the idea of "reason" so that only scientific reason counts, in a manner explicitly rejected by Locke with his idea of reason as "natural revelation," or as "the candle of the Lord."[18] For Dawkins, anything out of the reach of contemporary science is ruled

15 Richard Dawkins, *The God Delusion*, Bantam Press, London, p. 283.
16 Dawkins, *The God Delusion*, p. 282.
17 Dawkins, *The God Delusion*, p. 283.
18 Locke, *Essay Concerning Human Understanding*, Bk, IV, para 20, p. 280.

out, as is the idea that the power and validity of human reasoning could stem from a God who made us "in his image." That, however, is not the issue. The point is that one can espouse a belief with "passion" and still accept that one may be mistaken or perhaps only partially right. Good, groundbreaking scientists can spend their working lives balancing requisite scientific detachment with their personal commitment to a theory.

Some philosophers of religion, and not just those following the later Wittgenstein, think it a mistake to treat the content of religious belief on a par with scientific inquiry. Even with the caveat that transcendental reality is different from physical reality, they feel that the scientific model of truth distorts the character of religious belief too much. They would see it as a symptom of the dominance of scientific ways of thought on so-called analytic philosophy. For instance, John Cottingham says, "Seeing scientific thought as the paradigm to which all human cognition should aspire, many philosophers attempt to reduce religious language to a bald set of factual assertions whose literal propositional content is then to be clinically isolated and assessed."[19] He continues by suggesting that "the domain of religion is in certain respects more like the domains of art and literature and dreaming than it is like science."[20] He holds that approaching religion "with complete analytic detachment" may be a "stratagem of evasion," which involves a "flight from acknowledging all the dimensions of our humanity."[21]

Such criticism may warn of some dangers, but it introduces others. Certainly, genuine religion is not purely a matter of intellectual detachment or the testing of hypotheses with what Cottingham calls "the clinical dissection of phenomena."[22] It will involve our whole personality, and it may well tap into unconscious elements within us (as indeed the cognitive science of religion points out). We have seen how it involves passion and commitment. That may distinguish it at times from science, but the idea of science as some form of arid activity that its practitioners are not personally involved in may not do justice to the practice of science at its best.

19 John Cottingham, *The Spiritual Dimension*, Cambridge University Press, Cambridge, 2005, p. 71.
20 Cottingham, *The Spiritual Dimension*, p. 71.
21 Cottingham, *The Spiritual Dimensiom*, p. 71.
22 Cottingham, *The Spiritual Dimension*, p. 71.

Assimilating religion to art and literature may point out important features of how religion becomes involved with one's whole personality, but the comparison is still a dangerous one. Cottingham's reference to dreaming shows that. Even if the content of our dreams may be indicative of our characters and experiences, saying that religion is comparable to dreaming immediately can remove from it any right to claim truth. Dreams may tell us about a person. They cannot be relied on to give us proper information about anything else. Similarly, bringing in literature risks reducing religion again to the realm of story and myth, the antithesis of any claim to objective truth. It may be a mistake to think of religion as a matter of "intellectual sparring." It is an equal error to remove, or play down, its rational basis.

TENTATIVE BELIEF?

Claims to a truth, and the strength of one's commitment, can be logically separated. The issue, however, is not just that our commitment to beliefs may be misplaced simply because those beliefs could be proved to be mistaken. McKim suggested that the known fact of profound disagreement between religions is sufficient to weaken any initial assurance that a particular one is true. Yet, as we have seen in other spheres, disagreement should not of itself shake one's convictions if one believes one has good grounds for one's views and can produce them when challenged. There may be a question of why others will not accept what we do, but there can be many explanations for that, starting with their possible ignorance or lack of expertise.

Human life is no stranger to disagreement, in every walk of life and on every issue. Once we retreat to agnosticism or skepticism in the face of it, even in ordinary nonreligious spheres, the result will be paralysis and perhaps the nihilistic conclusion that nothing is true. A plurality of beliefs in a society may make it seem less cohesive. McKim, however, is not making this sociological point. For him, the issue is not just the progressive weakening of what might in previous ages have been seen as a necessary conformity to the dominant conventions. For him, the issue is a deeper epistemological one. He argues, "Disagreement about an issue or area of inquiry provides reason for whatever beliefs we hold about an issue or area of inquiry to be tentative. . . . Belief is tentative when it involves a recognition that one may be wrong about it, when it involves openness to revision and openness to inquiry."[23]

He carries this analysis quite far by suggesting this so-called critical stance in religion removes any possibility of "confident declaration."[24] McKim believes diversity, in all its forms, is "a challenge to orthodoxy,"[25] as well as to those who are confident in their rejection of all religion. He cheerfully accepts that "an implication of my position is that most martyrs who have died for their faith have been mistaken."[26] As that will presumably include the Crucifixion of Jesus, it is obvious that this is about more than the opening of religion to rational debate. It can become a challenge to the basic tenets of the Christian faith and presumably other faiths, as well. Tentative belief in the face of disagreement speedily slides into an inability to make any firm claims about what we do believe, let alone stand by them. The idea of orthodoxy has to be linked to ideas of truth. Once one is criticized, so is the other.

This notion of tentative belief is pursued to its logical conclusion when McKim suggests that "worship services and religious observances as currently constituted do not permit dissent, and this is their deepest flaw."[27] There should be a place for the rational discussion of difficulties of religious belief, and the difficulties could appear so great as to preclude any possibility of genuine worship. Yet that ability to examine claims to truth is different from the issue of real religious commitment and sincere worship. If faith is not merely a subjective matter but an attempt to lay hold of truth, that means it is vulnerable to error or the pangs of doubt. Even so, I still have to live my life in one way rather than another. Choices about commitments still have to be made even in an uncertain world. I always have to be committed to something, even if it is relativism or nihilism. The epistemological status of claims to truth is always distinct from issues about the firmness of my commitment.

Because faith is always faith in something or somebody, my beliefs can be expressed in propositional form. If I have faith in God, I must

23 McKim, *Religious Ambiguity and Religious Diversity*, p. 141.
24 McKim, *Religious Ambiguity and Religious Diversity*, p. 142.
25 McKim, *Religious Ambiguity and Religious Diversity*, p. 204.
26 McKim, *Religious Ambiguity and Religious Diversity*, p. 204.
27 McKim, *Religious Ambiguity and Religious Diversity*, p. 205.

believe that there is a God. My commitments are rationally based on that, and if I change my beliefs, I can no longer rationally keep to the same way of life. As we have already seen, there has been a tendency to downgrade the idea of religious faith and make it appear to be about the holder of it, rather than what it purports to refer to. This is part of the wider "privatization" of religion.[28] When any religion claims truth, it has to be of public, even universal, concern. If it is merely the expression of a personal commitment, made for reasons that are not interpersonally valid, it can be safely consigned to the category of the private, irrelevant, for instance, to issues of public policy. Notions of beliefs about truth then become subsumed in the general category of personal commitment. There can be no independent issue of the truth of my commitment. Doubting the truth of my beliefs, or wishing to test them, then, is made no different from becoming less committed. The propositional element of belief is ignored or actually denied.[29]

A further result is that my religious commitments will merely tell people about me. They may define who I am, and constitute my identity, because that is all they are, an expression of my personality or an indication of my cultural allegiances. All claims to truth have been abstracted from the situation. The idea of intellectual doubt, or even a willingness to listen to rational arguments against my beliefs, cannot then be separated from a lessening of commitment. Doubting, or even admitting the possibility of doubt, must imply the lessening of commitment. Rational argument about religious belief is made impossible.

Some religious believers may still see reason as the enemy of commitment. They may have too restricted a view about the capabilities of reason, or, more likely, they are demonstrating a fear about what reason may show. It bears repeating that if one thinks that one has recognized truth in whatever sphere, whether in science or religion or anywhere else, that should give confidence that reason will always uphold it, and apparently good arguments against it can be rationally undermined.

Religious diversity demonstrates that we are not all committed to the same truths or the same God. Any commitment is defined through the

---

28 See Roger Trigg, *Religion in Public Life: Must Faith Be Privatized?* Oxford University Press, Oxford, 2007.

29 See Roger Trigg, *Reason and Commitment*, Cambridge University Press, Cambridge, 1973.

expression of propositional beliefs on which it is implicitly, or explicitly, based. Otherwise religion will inevitably appear beyond the scope of rational debate and public concern, except as a potential irritant and source of conflict within society. Perhaps the word "diversity" itself suggests religion is not a matter of disagreement, as there is nothing to disagree rationally about. We diverge from each other but cannot disagree. Such a picture already sets the scene for various forms of conflict, within politics and beyond, that become issues of power and not reason.

THE SAME GOD?

What are religions in dispute about, as opposed to offering differing customs and ways of behaving? Can it even be said that they are all worshipping the same God, so that they can formulate disagreements about the character of the deity? The vast differences between, say, polytheism and monotheism would suggest that this is unlikely. We saw how Hick hankered after the idea that each religion, or least each religion worth bothering about, was about the same transcendent reality, the Real, even if it could not be characterized in a way that was not already specific to the insights of a particular religion. He is not alone, and if pluralism does not collapse into relativism, it has to assume that the "major" religions, however selected, do have some common core or common focus, however much they disagree in their characterizations.

We return to the idea that all, or many, religions may worship the same God without realizing it. Even the term "God" appears to narrow the idea of reality considerably. The recurring problem is that if religions have a similarity they are not conscious of, the doctrines and understandings of each must not be taken at face value. The propositional beliefs that seem to form the cores of their teachings do not represent the genuine content of the beliefs and have to be reinterpreted. They may even be seen as positively mistaken in their surface claims. When religion can simply be viewed as constituted by a commitment, issuing in a way of life, these questions can be avoided. The problem is no longer one of knowledge or reason. It becomes one of politics trying to get the different ways of life to coexist.

One way of identifying God is as the Creator of the universe and of all that is in it, including ourselves. That provides a unique purported reference. Yet Buddhism, for instance, does not talk of such a Creator, and so immediately that begins to narrow the field of religions and philosophies we are dealing with. The field has already been narrowed to exclude any polytheistic vision of the world in favor of one God as the source of everything. The temptation has often been to widen matters by abstracting from the idea of reality any notion of deliberate divine action. For example, the phrase derived from the theologian Paul Tillich, "the Ground of our Being,"[30] seems to abstract the idea of "ultimate reality" from any idea of active creation. Instead we appear to be left with some idea of reality as a passive object of human contemplation. That may seem more inclusive, but, again, it actually rules out notions of a Creator as central to religious faith. Instead of including more religious believers, it rules out many.

The pluralist program can only succeed in reconciling different religions by suggesting they are all concerned with the same reality if it makes a sustained attack on the significance of propositional beliefs cherished in specific traditions. Religions will have to be seen as bodies of commitment, and as ways of life, and not sustained and systematic attempts to claim truth. The motive could be the admirable one of trying to reduce apparent conflict and stress underlying agreement. That means showing that claims to truth are not what they seem, and the easiest way of doing that is to claim that religion is not about claiming truth at all.

This tendency can go very far indeed, to the point that historians and others can even come to discount the relevance of religious ideas as drivers of history. Religious beliefs are ignored because they do not seem to constitute the true reality of religion. As one historian of eighteenth-century America critically observes, in describing modern prejudices among academics, "Religion is treated as something cultural or social rather than as consisting of ideas and beliefs. Thus the new approach has tended to focus on ceremonies and ritual, community formation and individual experience, but not often on belief."[31] Given a propositional

---

30 Paul Tillich, *The Shaking of the Foundations*, Charles Scribner's Sons, New York, 1948, p. 53.
31 Nicholas P. Miller, *The Religious Roots of the First Amendment: Dissenting Protestants and the Separation of Church and State*, Oxford University Press, New York, 2012, p. 9.

element in religious commitment, any disagreement can raise the question as to whether people have different beliefs about the same God, worship different gods, or worship no god at all. Minor differences can lead people too easily to talk about "different religions," as when journalists use that phrase to describe the alleged divide between Catholics and Protestants in Northern Ireland. Such language may exacerbate divisions by exaggerating differences when both groups clearly worship the same God, and the Trinitarian God as portrayed by the traditional Christian creeds at that. A divergence of belief about the same God must be possible. Otherwise it will quickly become apparent that each individual worships a different God, because no one can have exactly the same understanding of his nature.

The problem is how far divergence can go before we wonder whether we are referring to the same deity. There must be limits. Zeus is not the Heavenly Father addressed by Jesus, and the concept of false religion must suggest that some worship false gods, or idols, that are illusory. That is certainly a traditional view, and it seems to make sense. Otherwise what is radically different and even aimed at supplanting previous beliefs wholesale will be said to be the same as them. When attempts are made to remove or add to the beliefs of a religion, the question has to be asked as to whether particular adherents still mean to refer to the same God as others.

How far can a religion be changed, or develop, while still being the same religion? This is a particular issue when new beliefs are formed against the background of the traditions of a long-lasting religion. Christianity grew out of Judaism. Islam was formed with a knowledge of both of those. Christian "heresies," such as Mormonism, add to Christianity in a significant way. At each stage, do different beliefs involve reference to a different God? It would seem odd to suggest that Jews and Christians do not worship the same God, and that when they each use the same words of the same Psalms they are praying to a different deity. The God of Abraham may or may not have been fully revealed in Jesus Christ, but the God who is referred to as the Creator in the book of Genesis is surely addressed by both Jews and Christians.

We must face the question of how much diversity of belief can still allow sameness of reference. The issue of identity across the divide between Christianity and Islam remains contentious. Do each worship the same God but possess radically different beliefs about Him? Is there any clear way of finally deciding? Monotheistic descriptions such as "Creator" may be held in common, and there may be a certain convergence in referring to the "God of Abraham." However, many Muslims find the doctrine of the Trinity so abhorrent that they think Christianity is a form of polytheism. They could on those grounds even deny that Christians do worship the one God.

These are complicated questions, but the point is that divergence of belief can begin to cast doubt about whether we are all referring to the same "object." That is why, in scientific theory, Thomas Kuhn famously suggested that after a radical transition from one scientific theory to another, such as the change from classical physics to quantum mechanics, "words change their meaning or conditions of applicability in subtle ways."[32] The suggestion is that words like "force," "mass," or "atom" may then be used so differently that, as Kuhn alleges, successive theories are "incommensurable." They can no longer be seen as different theories about the same objects, rather than theories positing radically different objects. This may, in his case, have been the path to an unacceptable relativism, but Kuhn is raising a crucial issue.[33]

The challenge is how far one's beliefs about a supposedly objective reality can change and still be about the same reality, as opposed to introducing a new one. Arguments about sense and reference have a long philosophical pedigree, and we need not enter into them now. The point is that beliefs about the nature of an object are relevant. Radical divergence in ways of referring to an object must raise the question of whether we are all still talking about the same thing. Whatever their intentions, different religions may not succeed in their identifications of the same reality if they cannot agree about any identifying description. This will be even more the case if they do not share the same history. Further, the various believers may not even be intending to talk about the same reality. If, for instance, there is one God who created the universe and all that there is, those who explicitly deny the possibility of such creation, or even the existence of one God, should not

---

32 T. S. Kuhn, "Reflections on My Critics," in *Criticism and the Growth of Knowledge*, ed. I. Lakatos and A. Musgrave, Cambridge University Press, Cambridge, 1970, pp. 266–267.

33 See Trigg, *Reason and Commitment*, pp. 99ff.

be understood as really talking about that. We would reach the absurd conclusion that total disagreement is, in fact, agreement.

This creates a problem. One writer puts it like this: "Since pluralist comparisons, like pluralist claims, posit basic equality between religious traditions, they challenge partisan attitudes, and suggest a shift from missionary activity to dialogue and sharing."[34] The implication is that no religion can claim superiority because none can claim more truth than the others. Pluralists typically think that they are all striving in the same direction, and, whatever their apparent beliefs, they are all concerned with the same ultimate reality. They may not succeed in referring to "it," but that, it seems, is what they are aiming at, and that gives the common ground necessary for dialogue, even if it may be in principle unknowable. To maintain this, the pluralist has to discount what the religious beliefs actually claim and substitute a vision of the ultimate that may not coincide with any of them. This is implausible if different commitments are defined in terms of the beliefs on which they are founded.

Beliefs matter. Specific ideas of what is true matter. However inconvenient this may be, we cannot dismiss them all or pretend they are about something different. If, on the other hand, we say that because there are so many competing views, they are probably *all* false, we are merely substituting another belief of our own about what is true. Even if we are right, that illustrates the crucial importance of what we each regard as true. The issue of truth simply can never be moved from the picture. Genuine mutual understanding between religions has to start from this fact. The content of religions cannot simply be revised or redefined without turning each of them into something they are not.

---

34 Garth Halett, *One God of All?* Continuum, New York, 2010, p. 117.

6

EDUCATION AND RELIGIOUS DIVERSITY

RELIGIOUS TRUTH IN EDUCATION

Religious commitments essentially involve an acceptance of certain propositions as true. Faith is itself always faith in something or somebody, imagined or real, and the moment it is specified what that is, beliefs are being articulated about what is real. It is not just an arbitrary attitude directed at a void, or an intention to live a particular way of life. That would make it difficult to see why there should be any particular respect for the principled stand a religious believer might wish to take. Conscientious objection typically cannot be just a matter of an idiosyncratic abhorrence of something. It depends, particularly when it is derived from religion, on a sincerely held belief about the nature of the world and what is right or wrong. Those who regard such attitudes as only subjectively valid cannot get to grips with why they are worthy of respect. The American legal philosopher Brian Leiter writes, "Notice that *beliefs* or the attitudes of *believers* are central to the analysis of religion precisely because it would be hard to see how mindless, habitual, or merely casual religious *practices* could claim whatever moral solicitude is due matters of *conscience*."[1] Actions that are mere rituals cannot be regarded as different from actions, compulsively repeated for no reason, such as the constant washing of already clean hands. They are left with no significance beyond themselves. Even if they are embedded in a way of life, they are ultimately pointless unless they can be given a purported grounding in some belief about why they matter.

---

1 Brian Leiter *Why Tolerate Religion?* Princeton University Press, Princeton, N.J., 2012, p. 35.

If religious practices make sense only against a given background of belief about what is true, they have to be answerable to human reason. We use our rationality to specify what we believe in, and thereby lay ourselves open to argument and even contradiction. Religion may sometimes seem to put itself beyond the scope of rational discussion, simply because it attempts to deal with the transcendent. Only those in the grip of an ideology that makes science the sole arbiter of reality see anything transcendent that as, by definition, inaccessible. The cognitive structure of the human mind is well equipped to conceive of it, as the cognitive science of religion well illustrates.

The perennial idea of faith as insulated from reason has to be constantly questioned. It is curious that Leiter himself stressed the importance of beliefs, as we have just seen, but had also just claimed that "religious beliefs, in virtue of being based on 'faith,' are insulated from ordinary standards of evidence and rational justification, the ones we employ in both common sense and science."[2] The old prejudices of verificationism keep on reappearing. Science itself nowadays often seems very far from common sense, as we saw when it was claimed by Robert McCauley that scientific belief is "unnatural" in a way that religious belief is not.

Any stress on beliefs that makes them impervious to reason inevitably leads to the dismissal of religious commitments as subjectively valid, or perhaps as a part of a way of life that itself could claim no external justification. Leiter removed the relevance of belief in the instant he had stressed it. What happens when we transfer this argument to the field of education? Even if beliefs can seem to matter in religion, the difficulty of arbitrating between different ones appears insuperable. For many decades now, the great fear in educational circles, particularly in the United Kingdom, has been that of indoctrination. It seems threatening, but all teaching is, in effect, indoctrination when it comes to imparting truth.

Pupils cannot be left to make up their own minds about what is true in physics. They must be taught there are agreed-on ideas of what is true in physics, and that there are acknowledged experts. No one can properly be left to decide for themselves what is true in such a context, because there are, it will be said, agreed-on standards of proof and evidence.

2 Leiter, p. 34.

Much that passes for knowledge at the frontiers of the subject may be more provisional than some would admit. Even so, students cannot make up their own minds about the physical constitution of the world without regard to inherited and contemporary wisdom. However, in the field of religion, in a divided society with plural beliefs about religion, teaching what is true will beg every question. Who is to decide what is true? What authority is being appealed to? The problem of living in a society that contains many diverse beliefs becomes stark.

It is generally agreed that parents can bring their children up as they wish and inculcate, by teaching and example, whatever beliefs, in religion and other areas, that they see fit. Article 26 of the Universal Declaration of Human Rights says explicitly that "parents have a prior right to choose the kind of education that shall be given to their children." What happens, however, when the children of many different kinds of family come together in one school? What are they then to be taught? Perhaps it should be what the State (with a capital letter) decides. No doubt a totalitarian regime would agree, but that is the problem.

What justifies a state, even a democratic one, imposing its own views on all children, regardless of family background? That would be the antithesis of democracy and the exercise of arbitrary authority. A democratic state may only act with the agreement of the majority, after due discussion, but this ignores the problem of diversity, and of religious diversity in particular. The dictatorship of the majority is a real threat in many societies. A religiously inclined majority might force their version of religion on reluctant minorities. In a secular society, the danger is also that religion is not given the value and attention that many parents would wish.

One answer is to provide different schools for different kinds of parents. In England, schools can be funded by the state but operated by the Church of England and the Roman Catholic Church, as well as, increasingly, other religious bodies, such as those of Jews, Muslims, and Hindus. This can avoid difficulty if parents have a genuine choice of type of school, although many are afraid that the policy could reinforce divisions in society. Social divisions only too apparent in Northern Ireland are often said to be reinforced by the existence of separate Protestant and Roman Catholic schools.

Such institutional divisions do not go to the heart of the epistemological challenge. How should religion be taught in any school, whatever its denominational allegiance? If Leiter is right and beliefs are at the core of any religion, it looks as if it is going to be very difficult to deal with them in schools, when reason is, by definition, excluded on the grounds that faith can have nothing to do with ordinary standards of evidence and rational justification. Divergent claims to truth cannot then in principle be rationally discussed. The temptation is to treat religion as a totally subjective matter in the classroom, as it often is in the wider public sphere. Some countries, such as the United States, proscribe the subject on the grounds of the separation of church and state. Countries that teach religious education, such as the United Kingdom, have a problem in a diverse society. One religion cannot be taught as true without antagonizing the others, so the tendency will be to treat religions as mere social facts. This will reinforce the temptation to view religions either as totally subjective or as ways of life. It may seem important that some basis of mutual understanding be established between the different religions, and that it starts with education. Speaking of truth, however, will appear divisive.

THE RELATIVIST TEMPTATION

One ensuing strategy in religious education is to concentrate on religious practices and describe them, much as an anthropologist might, without any commitment to justification. Religious festivals, such as Christmas, then become easy meat for description. However, because this can be done without discussion of the beliefs that might be thought to animate them, there arises a fundamental distortion of the purpose and point of religion. In the case of Christmas, Santa Claus, reindeer, and no doubt elves can loom larger than any idea of the mystery of the Incarnation, of God becoming man. Reference to the latter gets into contentious areas and raises the possibility of offending some parents.

Most religious practices can appear odd and pointless without the context of the beliefs that motivate them. Religion is trivialized when claims to truth are subtracted. However, once those claims take center stage, we need common standards of justification, and they are allegedly missing. Wittgenstein's approach to the philosophy of religion demands participation in a form of life, such as a religion, to understand it. The "insider" understands what an "outsider" cannot. One has to play a language-game to understand its rules. Practices then become more important than claims to truth are, and this can seem to be a way out of the difficulties of religious education. To an outsider, however, much can seem totally pointless without any grasp of the beliefs that animate practices.

How could "outsiders" get a grip on the nature of a religion? May the lack of understanding of a religion only be furthered by participation in its practices? That might be an argument for services of worship in schools. However, in a pluralist society, the provision of, for example, straightforward Christian worship, with hymns, prayers, and Bible readings, of the kind that British schools used to take for granted in a less fragmented society, may be increasingly problematic. Again the twin threats of indoctrination and offense to parents who are not Christian rear their heads.

In England, the Education Reform Act of 1988 made provision for collective worship that "shall be wholly or mainly of a broadly Christian character." The Act accepted that adjustments may have to be made in the light of the religious backgrounds of pupils, and provision was also made for pupils to be withdrawn from such worship at the wishes of their parents. Nevertheless, in the average community school, with a mixture of religious backgrounds and with staff who may not themselves be practicing Christians, the provision has become more difficult to implement. Nothing could illustrate more clearly the impact of a pluralist society on traditional education. The existence of shared beliefs and conventions can no longer be taken for granted.

The provision of religious education in such a climate has produced a perpetual tug-of-war between multi-faith and predominantly Christian emphases. This is all exacerbated by the continuing, unacknowledged influence of positivist, science-based views of truth. One educationalist writes of the problems arising "when one is aware that no religious claim to truth is in any way verifiable or falsifiable because there are no bases on which this could be judged."[3] He continues, "All natural laws are suspended in this fanciful land in which everything is possible if you can claim it happened.... Whatever is sufficiently supported has to be accepted in the public domain." As he says, not altogether reluctantly, this takes us in the direction of relativism, and it is hard to avoid the

---

3 Mark Chater and Clive Erricker *Does Religious Education Have a Future?* Routledge, London, 2013, p. 84.

conclusion that this is the direction that religious education in England has gone. Diversity is celebrated as an end in itself, to be respected. There has to be a fundamental dishonesty about this. If religions claim truth, that cannot be discounted. The relativist pretends to accept their claims, but then goes on to say that they are only true "for them." Doing so avoids any unseemly row between religions, or the disparagement of one set of beliefs from the standpoint of another. However, it reverts to the view that faith is purely subjective. The same writer refers to the basis on which truth claims are made, saying that they "can claim to be subjective or objective, but it is difficult to understand how religious claims can be the latter."[4] This means that they can only be a matter for an individual's subjective understanding or the agreement of a collective body, such as the Vatican Council, which enshrines them in doctrines. In either case, they have no validity for anyone aside from those who abide by them.

The understanding of religion as both a private matter for an individual and as a product of an agreed-on consensus by some group, however defined, puts it beyond criticism. All putative religion is on an equal footing and, if this position is held sincerely, must presumably be celebrated. There is a perpetual argument about which religions and ideologies should be included in religious education in England. The inclusion of humanism has been the subject of much discussion. Pushing religion into the private sphere, where it is not the subject of rational scrutiny or "public reason,"[5] means that all religions and similar belief systems have to be given equal respect, even when they appear to be contradicting each other, as in the case of humanism and religion. Each can escape all intellectual scrutiny. The most sophisticated theology becomes ranked with the most dangerous and irrational sects and superstitions. Indeed, the idea of a superstition fails to gain purchase as, in effect, all religion is placed in that category.

The paradox is that the demands of the British educational system make religion a public matter simply by insisting that it be taught in the classrooms of state schools. The dismissal of any possibility of public reason about religion goes hand in hand with the recognition that it has

4 Erricker, p. 86.
5 See my *Religion in Public Life, Must Faith be Privatized?* Oxford University Press, Oxford, 2007.

to be dealt with publicly. Often this is in the name of social cohesion and the official hope that religious education can be used for forms of social engineering. It can then be a force for mutual understanding and comprehension between different religious communities. The consequence is that anything promoting division is frowned on. Competing claims to truth certainly fall into that category.

There are costs for this approach. We have just mentioned that all religions have to be accepted equally. The word "equality" is usually coupled with that of "diversity." This means that all religion is presented in a positive light and that, as one educationalist puts it, "there is a lack of scrutiny given to the rational incoherence and unacceptable practices of some religious forms."[6] Proponents of relativism, and those liberals who see no place for religious argument in the public square, face a problem. They may not want to get into doctrinal disputes with members of a particular religion, and they may find it politic not to condemn religion as such, or whole swathes of it. Nevertheless, everyone has to accept that, by any reasonable standard, there are bad forms of religion. Some religions have encouraged child sacrifice and may still do so. Many other horrendous practices have been undertaken in the name of one religion or another. There is, in other words, a pathology of religion. Some may see all religion as harmful, but even they have to accept that some are more harmful than others. The "feeble" English clergyman derided by Wittgenstein is not in the same category as a suicide bomber, thinking he is dying for his faith.

Without the possibility of rational discussion and scrutiny and the operation of critical faculties, all religion has to be accepted at face value or all has to be dismissed. We seem to have a choice between the old-fashioned positivism that holds religion in contempt but also cannot properly account for the theoretical entities of physics, and the acceptance of a mentality of "anything goes" that must go hand in hand with relativism. The result in British religious education has to be an uneasy and superficial acceptance of religion as a social fact, together with an unfocused hope that somehow religious education can be an instrument for promoting tolerance and respect for difference. This must all somehow be accomplished without becoming entangled with what many believers would consider the heart of their religion, namely that

6 Erricker, p. 87.

it claims a truth worthy of universal attention. That is what Christians and Muslims believe, to take just two examples, but neither scientific naturalism nor relativism can accept it.

CAN RELIGIOUS EDUCATION SUCCEED IN A PLURALIST SOCIETY?

What can religious education hope to achieve in a pluralist society? In the Britain of the 1950s, there was no doubt about it. Pupils were taught scripture and were introduced to Christian doctrine. A society that was at least nominally Christian wanted to pass on knowledge of its inherited beliefs. This helped provide a common cultural background, whether or not it increased religious faith. Scripture, however, became generalized into "religious knowledge" and, as confidence in the truth claims of religion lessened, that became transmuted into "religious education." Terms such as "religious studies" – a more obviously sociological title – or even "philosophy" or "ethics" are gaining ground. Not only does this exhibit uncertainty about the purpose of religious education, but there is also clearly embarrassment that religion should be given any privileged place at all. Why, it may be asked, should a religious worldview be given any more attention than a non-religious worldview?

There is continuing philosophical confusion about the place of religious education in a pluralist society. Some societies, such as the United States and France, banish religion from the classroom. This is still the subject of much controversy in the former, but is less controversial in France with its avowed secular policy of *la laicité*, keeping the public square free of all religion and religious symbolism. Yet even there, a report to the French President on the continuation of the policy accepted that in schools "a better mutual understanding of different cultures and traditions of religious thought is today essential."[7] The report recommended that the study of religion be integrated into the teaching of other subjects, such as history. It certainly saw that pretending that religions do not exist is not conducive to good education, while insisting that it was important to give full respect to *la diversité spirituelle*. Even

---

7 *Laicité et Republique, Rapport au President de la Republique*, La Documentation Francaise, Paris 2004, p. 137.

so, religious schools flourish in the private sector in France, as parents try to escape formal state neutrality in religion.

One pathway for religious education, either as a subject in itself or in conjunction with other disciplines, is simply to teach what the different world religions stand for. It is acknowledged that increasing religious diversity in England has been the prime motivating factor. A trailblazer in 1975 was the Birmingham Agreed Syllabus for Religious Education. It is no coincidence that this grew out of the same diverse social background in the same English city at the same time as did John Hick's pluralism. Gaining factual information of this kind should certainly promote understanding at a certain level. Yet this kind of factual teaching is regarded with disdain by many proponents of religious education. As one proponent writes, "the teaching of [religious education] as facts necessarily precludes the possibility of debate."[8] He regards the teaching of "facts" as "particularly baneful because it would create advantages for those who want their own religious truths to be taught as facts."

This puts a premium not on imparting knowledge, of whatever kind, but on getting individual pupils to make up their own minds, presumably from a position of great ignorance. This stems from an atomistic view of individuals separated from community or social background but able, somehow, to form judgments in a total vacuum. It is a paradox that one of the strong narratives impelling English religious education is the need to further social cohesion through giving equal respect to all beliefs. However, encouraging people to make up their own minds in this way itself suggests a myriad of unrelated atoms without any interest in cohering with others or any need to do so. The stress on subjective decision making corrodes any notion of a community or of a society with any shared beliefs.

This may be pupil-centered, but it also tilts the scales to a subjectivism, according to which each individual is encouraged to construct truths for themselves. The communal aspects of religion are discounted, as is any cultural inheritance. The attainment targets of religious education have been, since 1994 in England and Wales, "learning about" and "learning from." This suggests continued ambivalence about the purpose of religious education in a pluralist society. Is it to inform

8 Erricker, p. 133.

pupils of the content of different religions, is it to help them form their own worldviews, or is it, perhaps, to encourage moral behavior through the imparting of uplifting stories, such as that of the Good Samaritan, outside of the religious context that gives them meaning?

There also seems to be a systematic inability to distinguish between teaching what others believe to be true and teaching the beliefs of a religion as true. However, it should certainly be possible to teach what Christians believe to be true in a fair but neutral manner without any judgment as to whether they are right. It is possible to teach what the Bible says without coercing atheists into accepting any of it for themselves. Yet in a diverse society, it may seem invidious to pick out one sacred text among many and give it particular attention. Far better, it may seem, to concentrate on the needs of individual children, rather than to bore them with abstruse ideas in difficult texts. One educationalist says, "What makes religious education relevant in the school curriculum is that it is personal, interpersonal and contemporary."[9] Religion is reduced to what individual pupils can relate in their own lives at a particular time, and becomes a matter for their own personal interpretation. What is right for them is right for them. Such subjectivism certainly allows for respect for diversity, which is one of the main objectives of English religious education. No one can say that another's judgment is wrong.

A genuine relativism, however misguided, is at least consistent with a society passing on its beliefs and culture to the next generation, regarding them as constitutive of the identity of a society. An avowedly Christian society could pass on its beliefs through its schools because that is the kind of society it was. On that basis, Christianity could be taught in English schools not because it was true in some objective sense that had to be recognized the world over. Rather it would be taught because it was, through historical development, part of what it is to be English (or British). Religion can often be caught up intimately with national identity, and the erosion of Christian belief as a feature of British society appears to be one factor challenging the social cohesion of the country.

Even a proponent of a science-based atheism such as Richard Dawkins regrets what he terms "the biblical ignorance displayed by

---

9 Mike Castelli, "Faith Dialogue as A Pedagogy for a Post-Secular Religious Education," *Journal of Beliefs and Values* 13, 2012, pp. 207–216. 215.

people educated in more recent decades than I was."[10] He gives examples of how biblical allusions in many forms of literature are lost and we are then cut off from our cultural inheritance. The same can be said of our musical and artistic inheritance. Much classical music and the great paintings of past centuries become incomprehensible without a recognition of their provenance in Christianity. Members of an audience for a performance of Handel's *Messiah* might now be puzzled about its meaning and its origin.

Relativism underwrites the continuation of a culture but collapses when it can no longer be defined geographically or politically. A society then becomes so diverse that it begins to break into separate societies, even if they coexist in the same space. A major and recurring issue is precisely how the society to which beliefs relate is to be defined. If major religious disagreement itself comes to determine the boundaries of a society or culture, there is the recurring danger of circularity. The truths of beliefs are confined to a particular society, but the society is defined by the fact that its members have those beliefs. In the end we are saying little more than that some people have those beliefs, and we are still left with the problem of situating the truth that is claimed.

The travails of English religious education are a particular example of a broader problem. As we have seen, it can be avoided, as in the United States, by refusing to deal with it in the classroom. However, it is artificial to suppose that religion can be abstracted from the study of human affairs without distortion. American history is often unintelligible without looking at the influence of religion. Even a study of the U.S. Constitution itself has to raise the subject, not least because the Constitution enjoins the "free exercise of religion." What is it that thus has to be protected, and why does it deserve such special attention? These are not trivial issues.

DOES CELEBRATING DIVERSITY HELP RELIGIOUS FREEDOM?

The importance of freedom of religion lies at the root of much of the current emphasis on respect for diversity and the equality of religions. In the context of freedom of religion, the Toledo Principles were drawn up

10 Richard Dawkins, *The God Delusion*, Bantam Press, London, 2006, p. 340.

on a European basis by the Organisation for Security and Cooperation in Europe (OSCE) to provide recommendations for how teaching about religion and beliefs in schools could proceed. The group drawing them up was motivated by the consideration "that it is important for young people to acquire a better understanding of the role that religions play in today's pluralistic society."[11] They held that ignorance "increases the likelihood of misunderstanding, stereotyping and conflict." Thus, teaching about religions would ameliorate this. Yet they also stressed as a fundamental principle that "there is a positive value in teaching that emphasizes respect for *everyone's* right to freedom of religion and belief."[12]

Respecting, and even promoting, diversity as an end in itself is different from promoting respect for basic human rights such as religious freedom. The Toledo Principles state that "the right to freedom of religion or belief is a universal right and carries with it an obligation to protect the rights of others, including respect for the dignity of all human beings."[13] Celebrating diversity as an end in itself is rootless and unprincipled. There must be limits to the diverse beliefs we are willing to acknowledge and even encourage. What about those who want to coerce everyone else to accept their own stance? Respect for diversity cannot stretch that far without undermining itself. On the other hand, given a general respect for freedom, diversity of belief may seem an inevitable result, whether or not we welcome all its manifestations. The difference between the two positions is that simply accepting diversity and the equality of all beliefs does not give us any place secure to stand. When all beliefs are of equal value and diversity is intrinsically good, it is impossible to hold any principled position on the grounds that it is true and deserves universal recognition. A belief in the importance of human freedom, including freedom of religion, requires much more than some idiosyncratic commitment.

The Toledo Principles combine freedom of religion with rights, bringing in the idea of universal human rights deserving universal recognition. Significantly, they refer to human dignity. This is different from simply

---

11 *Toledo Guiding Principles on Teaching About Religions and Beliefs in Public Schools*, OSCE, (Organisation for Security and Cooperation in Europe), 2007, p. 9.
12 *Toledo Guiding Principles*, p. 12.
13 *Toledo Guiding Principles*, p. 14.

upholding diversity, and continually raises the question of what justifies talk of the intrinsic value of all human beings. Some would make such talk simply a form of secular religion, but that alone does not explain its rational basis. Others point out that such ideas are firmly grounded in theistic principles, such as that we are all made in the image of God. Other explanations and justifications might be offered.

The problem is that we cannot properly assume the validity of talk of human rights and human dignity without grounding it in some way. We need to stand somewhere with substantive beliefs about the world and the place of humans in it. The passive acceptance of many diverse beliefs, coupled with a reluctance to criticize any beliefs publicly or in a classroom, produces a vacuum. In that vacuum all kinds of coercive and recognizably irrational views may flourish.

The benign acceptance of all beliefs can unintentionally allow intolerant forms of belief to fester unchallenged. Treating religious differences as if they were a matter for subjective preference, to be decided by individuals according to their own tastes, undermines the possibility of religion (and antireligious views) claiming truth. The indiscriminate respect for diversity that can flourish in religious education paradoxically removes any understanding of the seriousness and importance of difference. Religions are not trivial lifestyle choices, chosen for personal reasons out of reach of scrutiny in the public sphere. There may be more underlying agreement between various religions than sometimes appears, but they cannot all be wholly right.

Well-meaning educationalists and others, in their search for social cohesion rather than division, find this disturbing. They do not want to be put in the position of indoctrinating, of ramming the truth claims of one religion down the throats of adherents to another, although there may at the same time be an unquestioning acceptance of the rhetoric of human rights. Far safer, it may seem, to celebrate diversity. That means, if we are to be consistent, that we may find ourselves acknowledging beliefs that hold ideas of tolerance and respect in total contempt. Teachers cannot uphold tolerance, respect for others, the importance of religious freedom, and other democratic values without implicitly ruling out alternative views and, in effect, preaching. It looks as if some diversity might be acceptable and other forms not. Democratic values matter, but perhaps the unintended implication is that issues of religious truth do not. As we have continually seen, the underlying paradox of

pluralism is that, unless it descends into relativism, it has to rule something out. Accepting diverse beliefs has to rest on a generally valid principle, such as that of freedom of religion. Pluralism can never escape
ultimately having to take the logical form of an exclusivist position.
Not everything can be accepted.

Accepting all belief systems may be impracticable and ultimately
impossible in a country that wishes to uphold democracy. The underlying failure to take claims to truth seriously produces a further danger.
When children are presented with differing practices and beliefs, none
of which is given priority, an indifference to all religion can easily be
bred, which turns into outright cynicism about whether any religion
matters. In several Western countries, such as England and France,
Muslim parents sometimes prefer to send their children to a Catholic
or other denominational school. That could be because they prefer a
school in which religion is taken seriously, rather than a secular state
school where "neutrality" turns into opposition to all religion.

Richard Dawkins illustrates the problem when arguing for atheism
in *The God Delusion*. He accepts that there may be a case for teaching
about religions, just as he accepts that the ignorance of the Bible is to
be deplored from a cultural point of view. He then quotes a critic of
multi-faith education who says that "'children these days are taught
that all religions are of equal worth, which means that their own has no
special value.'" Dawkins responds, "'Yes indeed: that is exactly what it
means. Well might this spokesman worry.'"[14] Dawkins goes on to point
out that faiths are mutually incompatible, which is why their various
adherents consider their own superior. They all cannot be superior to
each other. Dawkins's own conclusion is that this all goes to show that
none of them can claim any validity.

It is central to education to lead children to think critically and reason
for themselves, but schools are understandably reluctant to undermine
the religious beliefs in which students are brought up. Dawkins[15] is
critical of the tolerance shown by the United States Supreme Court[16]
toward the Amish practice of withdrawing their children from high

14 Dawkins, p. 340.
15 Dawkins, p. 330.
16 For a full discussion of this case, see Roger Trigg, *Religion in Public Life*, Oxford
   University Press, Oxford 2007, p. 57ff.

school. He goes on to proclaim that "there is something breathtakingly condescending, as well as inhuman, about the sacrificing of anyone, especially children, on the altar of 'diversity' and the virtue of preserving a variety of religious traditions."[17] He thus welcomes religious diversity as a stick with which to beat religion, but deplores respect for it. It certainly seems unacceptable in a democratic society that schools should endorse, even by implication, the hard-edged atheism that Dawkins advocates. They would then be as guilty of indoctrination as they would be if they taught the Bible as true.

OBJECTIVITY AND NEUTRALITY

Everyone responsible for education in schools have to accept that, if it is in some sense natural for children to see things in a religious way, religion cannot be banished totally from the classroom. One way of approaching the issue in Western schools could be for a school to begin by teaching about Christian beliefs and, when children are older, introduce them to other religions. This would ensure that they have a grounding in one religion, namely that which formed their own culture. With greater pluralism, it is inevitable that this approach will be challenged. In Norway, a landmark case,[18] initiated by Norwegian humanists, went to the European Court of Human Rights, producing a judgment that questioned the concentration on Christianity in traditional Norwegian teaching.

The Grand Chamber of judges came to their decision narrowly by nine votes to eight. This illustrated how controversial the whole issue can be. The decision of a single judge had an effect on the future cultural trajectory of Norway. The majority accepted that paying more attention to Christianity than other religions was reasonable, given Norway's history and culture, but stressed their objection to "not only quantitative but even qualitative differences applied to the teaching of Christianity as compared to that of other religions."[19] Their conclusion was that Norway "did not take sufficient care that information and knowledge

---

17 Dawkins, p. 331.
18 See also Roger Trigg *Equality, Freedom and Religion*, Oxford University Press, Oxford 2012, p. 60ff.
19 *Folgero v. Norway*, Grand Chamber, European Court of Human Rights, Strasbourg, June 29, 2007, No: 15472/02, para. 95.

included in the curriculum be conveyed in an objective, critical and pluralistic manner."[20]

"Pluralism" here signifies more than the acknowledgment of, and even respect for, those who hold different religious and antireligious views. It carries with it the desire that schools should be neutral about all such views and should deal with them objectively. The danger in this is that in the face of radical disagreement about religion, questions of truth are shirked so that claims to truth do not seem to matter any more. However, as we have already indicated, there is a distinction between teaching what Christianity holds to be true and preaching it as true. As children get older, it should be easier for them to discuss various claims in a philosophical and critical manner. Courses in the philosophy of religion have become very popular with sixteen- and seventeen-year-olds in English schools. They are often less effective than they might be because of the ignorance of many students at that age of what Christianity, let alone other religions, stands for. Their critical faculties can be blunted because they have been left with little material to be critical about.

The need for objectivity has produced a fear of dealing in any way with claims to truth. Objectivity is made to imply not a passion for truth in all disciplines, but a detachment from all possible truth claims in controversial areas. That is why truth claims in religion are often presented as mere myths or stories, with a stress on the individual pupil interpreting them as best suits the individual. Yet disagreements between citizens about religion and battles about what can be properly taught in state schools are political issues. They should not require philosophical conclusions. How do we arrive at agreement about such matters? How can people of different religions, and none, live together so that a society does not splinter into component groups living apart from each other? These are always difficult issues, but they are not arguments about the philosophical status of religion. Adopting certain philosophical understandings of religion may appear to help escape from difficulties about religious disagreement. The importance of mutual understanding and social cohesion takes priority.

The fear, however, of many is that objectivity and neutrality can breed ambivalence about all religion. We have seen that parents may

---

20 *Folgero,* para. 102.

have good cause to be worried that, when confronted with many religions on an equal footing, their children may be tempted to dismiss them all. The ensuing idea of relativism can be corrosive of belief. These worries were crystallized in a case brought by parents in Quebec. A 2005 Act had replaced Catholic and Protestant programs of instruction with a secular one on 'Ethics and Religious Culture'. The principles underlying this were the familiar ones of "state neutrality"[21] toward religions and the need for "objective presentation of various religions"[22] to children so as not to put them in an "obligatory and coercive situation." The Court stated that "given the religious diversity of present-day Quebec, the state can no longer promote a vision of society in public schools that is based on the historically dominant religions."[23] The parents concerned objected that they were not going to be allowed to have their children exempted from the new "Ethics and Religious Culture" (ERC) course, and considered that this infringed their freedom of religion. The nub of their objection was that "students following the ERC course would be exposed to a form of relativism which would interfere with the appellants' ability to pass on their faith to their children."[24]

The Canadian Supreme Court ruled against the parents, partly because they made their objection before the course had actually started, so their fears could not be proven to have been valid. The Court held that "the suggestion that exposing children to a variety of religious facts in itself infringes their religious freedom or that of their parents amounts to a rejection of the multicultural reality of Canadian society."[25] The problem lies in what is to count as a religious fact. Diverse religious claims to truth might themselves present difficulties for those proposing a policy of multiculturalism, where all are equal and all beliefs are to be treated equally. The category of objective truth in religion can then be challenged and disregarded. It becomes easier to talk of the disparate practices of different religions, and the superficialities of different festivals. It looks as if this was proving a temptation for the proposed

---

21 *S.L et al v. Commission Scolaire des Chenes et al.* (2012 SCC7, 426 N.R. 2012, 352–383), para. 10.
22 *S.L et al*, para. 5.
23 *S.L et al*, para. 1.
24 *S.L et al*, para. 29.
25 *S.L et al*, para. 40.

course. Indeed, one of the judges commented that future implementation of the program could possibly infringe the rights of the appellants, although that still had to be seen.[26] He asked, by way of illustration of his point, "Does the content of the Christmas-related exercises for six year old students encourage the transformation of an experience and tradition into a form of folklore?"

The battle between different parental desires for their children's education can be hard to resolve in a pluralist society. Keeping religion out of schools completely is one solution but not altogether realistic, given the centrality of religion in human life. It is liable to creep back through subjects such as history and politics, to name just two. Another possible path to solve the problem is for the state to provide different schools for different religions. This meets fears of a loss of religious and cultural identity by raising fears of a breakdown of social cohesion. Yet in Quebec even private denominational schools were not given any right to exercise religious freedom, when faced with the requirements of the province. A Roman Catholic High School in Montreal was compelled to teach the ERC course from the 'neutral', secular perspective demanded. That decision was upheld by the Quebec Court of Appeal,[27] and the matter was then taken top the Canadian Supreme Court.

Behind these political and legal concerns lie unresolved issues about the essential features of any religion. If claims to the truth of its beliefs are simply swept aside as unworthy of rational discussion, within the classroom or outside, the religion itself is ultimately being devalued. In a diverse society, differences must be taken seriously and judged in their own terms if they are to be truly respected.

26 LeBel J. S. L. at al. para. 58.
27 *Quebec v. Loyola High School*, 2012 QCCA 2139.

7

TRUTH AND COERCION

INTOLERANCE OR HUMILITY?

Many find it threatening that religions can make "objective" claims to truth that apply universally. This may be because the alleged truth in question is not just of marginal importance, or of interest to a few specialists. By definition, it could concern all humanity, and the place of humans in the scheme of things. If, in addition, the religion concerned considers that recognizing such truth appears important for the eternal destiny of each person, it might follow that everyone should be informed of this, so as to have a chance of living in accordance with that truth. There could appear to be a positive duty of proselytizing.

Christianity and Islam both believe they have a universal message. If there is one God, one would expect that He would be regarded as the God of all people, and not just some. Even in the Old Testament, the God of Israel is also often seen as the God of the whole world, so that one day "all nations" will acknowledge Him.[1] The universalist message is muted, however, in comparison with the deliberate offering of the Christian message to Gentiles as well as Jews in the New Testament.

Even so, a constant theme in the Old Testament is that the Jews must serve "the Lord your God" alone, and "must not go after other gods, gods of the nations around you."[2] Indeed, if there is one God, maker of heaven and earth, that is only to be expected. Monotheism insists that all reality, including that of God, is the same for everybody, whatever their beliefs. One religion cannot live in one world, and another in another.

---

[1] See Gerald O'Collins, *Salvation for All: God's Other Peoples*, Oxford University Press, 2008.

[2] Deuteronomy 6:14.

There is only one world, one version of reality. Monotheism can have no truck with relativism, or alternative gods. Beliefs may construct gods, but those who believe in one God cannot allow for other parallel deities, even in the sense that other people have their gods while monotheists look to their one deity. Monotheism must not only imply the falsity of all other alleged gods, but, if it is true to itself, it has to proclaim it to all, loud and clear. Otherwise, by definition, it is not monotheism, or even realism, but allows for different kinds of gods, according to the varying nature of people's beliefs. Not surprisingly, this proclamation of universal truth can create resentment and opposition. People do not like being told they are wrong when they perceive this to be an attack on their most cherished beliefs.

Monotheism characteristically depends on a form of metaphysical realism. Its universal applicability is intimately connected with the view of a reality that holds whether people acknowledge it or not. The one God must be all-powerful, and not in competition with other sources of power. As Creator, such a God will be supreme, and self-subsistent, not dependent on anything or anybody. Such a God cannot be dependent on the beliefs of human beings, without a deep contradiction emerging between His alleged independence and power, and the fact that He only appears to exist because humans believe He does. One cannot properly worship, or pray to, what is simultaneously acknowledged to be a reflection of human thinking.

Monotheism could find it difficult to be tolerant of alternative belief systems, particularly if they posit other gods. This is still the case even if monotheists are fully accepting of the adherents of other faiths themselves. Different beliefs about the divine nature may still be seen as mistaken, and attempts to posit several gods will be regarded with horror. If there is one God, one Ultimate Reality, as the ground of everything, there can only be one source of truth. The one God has to set the standard, as is tacitly indicated in loose secular references to the fact that "God only knows," or to the philosophical impossibility of seeking a "God's-eye view."

There is the possibility for trouble in all this. Monotheistic faiths, with their vision of one form of truth, can be intolerant of competitors. The belief in an objective reality that rules out many religious beliefs as not just wrong but perhaps even wicked can be viewed as setting up an apparent basis for religious intolerance, if not direct persecution.

The temptation of relativism is that it can appear to be a source of toleration. There is then no external standpoint in principle from which others can be judged adversely. We are all equally in the same position.

This may express to the realist a problem of the human condition. We are all trapped within the preconceptions of our inherited forms of understanding, both as humans and as members of one society or another. Yet there may still be a reality beyond us that we may aspire to understand. The difficulties in our way should give us cause for humility. We do not know everything, and we should be ready to talk seriously to those with a different vision. That does not mean there is no such thing as being right or being mistaken, but that we should avoid the arrogance of assuming too easily that we ourselves are right.

Rowan Williams, writing when he was Archbishop of Canterbury, wanted to stress the importance of truth for a Christian, but adds that "there is a proper kind of humility which, even as we proclaim our conviction of truth . . . obliges us to acknowledge with respect the depth and richness of another's devotion to and obedience to what they have received as truth." He continues by saying that "we have none of us received the whole truth as God knows it; we all have things to learn."[3]

There is a fine line between lapsing into a seemingly tolerant relativism that accepts all beliefs and arrogantly asserting the truth of our own beliefs. The former way fails to take seriously the fact of religious difference, and the latter suggests that we already know everything. The problem is how far it is possible to balance a full commitment to the truth of one's beliefs, perhaps to the extent of dying because of them, as so many martyrs have done, with a recognition of our less than full understanding of what is true. People have often found it difficult to separate the two. Robert McKim is able to pass quickly from the idea of a proper mystery in religious belief to that of agnosticism, writing: "The dominant characteristic in faith ought to be hope, or exploration, rather than certitude. . . . Mystery requires a more modest, more agnostic, faith."[4]

The problem is how we can be humble about beliefs when faced with devout believers of other religions, but not lapse into agnosticism

3 Rowan Williams, *Faith in the Public Square*, Bloomsbury, London, 2012, p. 301.
4 Robert McKim, *Religious Ambiguity and Religious Diversity*, Oxford University Press, Oxford, 2001, p. 124.

and a half-hearted commitment, or no commitment at all. There is an undoubted attraction about an approach that takes seriously the fact of an objective reality but questions our own full grip on knowledge of that reality. It can carry with it certain virtues, in contrast to the perceived dogmatism of those who think they have full and secure knowledge. Yet the picture of the tolerant believer who holds very lightly to his beliefs does not ring true as a description of ordinary religious belief. If truth matters, religious believers, like others, will care deeply about what is true. This may certainly motivate such people to listen to others, but, as we have seen, believing something to be true does not necessarily involve detachment and indifference.

The obverse of what McKim is saying is that religious belief, as normally constituted and expressed, is likely to be intransigent, and hostile to examination. In the face of that assumption, Williams's plea for humility and mutual respect may seem highly optimistic. Yet those who find most to respect in the deep devotion and commitment of believers in another religion are often those who are mostly deeply committed to the truth of their own. This may seem paradoxical, but it is not fanciful to have a fellow feeling for those who care deeply about religious truth when one does oneself, even if their beliefs are very different. If, as has been maintained, beliefs about what is true must be logically separate from the commitment one gives to it, one can still respect the commitment while not agreeing about the alleged truths on which it is based.

Religion may still be accused of being a distinctive source of division and strife. It may seem intrinsically intolerant because of its insistence on being fully committed to a truth that applies to others even though they explicitly reject it. If, however, believers ought only to hold, and express, their beliefs in a tentative manner, ideas of preaching and conversion would have to be thrown into question. Proselytizing is often a source of resentment among those it is aimed at, and that, too, is characteristic of some religions. The fear of indoctrination in education is mirrored in the wider world by the constant fear of forms of coercion and means of persuasion by those who try to deal with those with whom they disagree. Extreme examples of attempted coercion through the tactics of terror, by the adherents of one religion confronted with competitors, are only too prevalent in some parts of the contemporary world. Given the history of some forms of religion, together with these more recent manifestations, religion's "absolutist" tendencies are still viewed by some with suspicion.

THE INQUISITION AND "ABSOLUTISM"

The later European Enlightenment in such places as France wanted to supplant what its proponents regarded as authoritarian religion with reason. Religion, particularly in this case the Roman Catholic Church, was seen as an oppressive enemy of human freedom. Nothing better illustrated the way in which the Catholic Church tried to maintain and enforce its vision of truth than the notorious Inquisition. Essentially a mechanism for purging the Church of dangerous or "false" beliefs, it came to epitomize the imposition of cruel and arbitrary punishment. Created in the thirteenth century, it survived in various forms into the nineteenth century.[5] It was not, for example, abolished on Malta until Napoleon came on the scene. Although the Spanish Inquisition was the best known, it flourished elsewhere across Southern Europe and in the territories of the Spanish and Portuguese empires. The Inquisition was established in Mexico in 1570. It was known everywhere for its inhuman methods, including torture, and the constant threat of execution. Executions were carried out in the Iberian Peninsula until the end of the eighteenth century.[6] Yet although the procedures of the Inquisition were minutely regulated and documented, it became increasingly seen as monstrously unjust. Its procedures were secret, and judicial action could be based on one witness. The accused "could not know the names of their denouncers or of the witnesses for the prosecution, or the time and place of the crimes imputed to them."[7]

What drove this whole bureaucratic machine, and how could it last for so many centuries across such a wide area? Its object was the imposition of orthodoxy, according to the beliefs of the Roman Catholic Church, and the stamping out of any apparently false belief that threatened it. Witchcraft, magic, and other forms of superstition were fair game, but what gave the Inquisition motivation in many places was the

---

5 See Francisco Bethencourt, *The Inquisition: A Global History, 1478–1834*, Cambridge University Press, Cambridge, 2009.
6 Bethencourt, *The Inquisition*, p. 436.
7 Bethencourt, *The Inquisition*, p. 369.

spread of Protestantism on the one hand and the fear of the influence of Islam and Judaism on the other. In both cases what was at issue was the weakening of the authority of the Church and its control of what could be regarded as true. "The Iberian tribunals," we are told, "initially concentrated on prosecuting the crimes of Islamism and Judaism."[8] That is significant because many in the Iberian Peninsula had converted, willingly or not, from those religions, and were suspected of being less than whole-hearted "New Christians."

The methods and cruelty of the Inquisition have made the very word one of abuse ever since. Yet the idea of truth, in a warped way, dominated the whole process. Everything was geared to make the accused repent, confess their heresy, and be received back into the fold of the Church. In Spain and Portugal the culmination of the secret trials was a public spectacle and procession, called significantly the *auto-da-fe*, the "act of faith," which centered on the presentation of the accused in large numbers at a great ceremony, and their division into those who were penitent and those found guilty and condemned to death. The decisions of the Inquisition and the fates of the individuals accused were not known until this public presentation of the results of the investigations. The condemned were handed over to the civil authorities and taken to a public pyre for burning. The penitents took part in the "abjuration," that is, "the public and formal expression of the repentance of the penitent, the rejection of heresies and renewed commitment to the Church."[9] As it was considered that their immortal destiny was at stake, this penitence was a cause of thanksgiving by the Church for the victory won over the "impious." Truth had been vindicated.

A strong belief in the objectivity of truth, coupled with a sincere belief that it was in the interest of "heretics" to be brought back to the true Faith and the one Church, could be said to be the root of all this. The obvious solution might be to deny that there is such a thing as truth, so that there can be no valid reason for imposing one's own beliefs on those who disagree. This view might be reinforced by the observation that a nonreligious insistence on objective truth can itself result in totalitarian persecution. Lenin preached a materialist philosophy as objectively true, and thought, like other Marxists, that this

---

8 Bethencourt, *The Inquisition*, p. 321.
9 Bethencourt, *The Inquisition*, p. 277.

gave a justification for overriding individual freedom in the supposed interests of the proletariat.[10]

Not surprisingly, the Inquisition roused a tremendous revulsion in Northern Europe, which still lives on. Its extreme and colorful Spanish form was particularly reviled, but the so-called Roman Inquisition, directed from Rome, could be just as ruthless in rooting out alleged heresy. This, however, was not a wholesale attempt to force people of other religions into the Christian fold. The Inquisition was attempting to "purify" the Church and enforce discipline on its own baptized members. Some of them may have entered the Church, voluntarily or through coercion, from other religions and were accused of backsliding. What was missing, however, was any idea of respecting freedom of conscience. Truth had to be acknowledged and obeyed.

This basic idea that once one is a member of a religion, through baptism, birth, or whatever, one cannot leave it lives on in different contexts in the contemporary world. One should not, it seems, question or deny an objective truth that has been already been accepted. It is difficult, or impossible, to convert from Islam to, say, Christianity in many Muslim countries. There is a basic dynamic of not allowing the rejection of a truth once accepted. "Apostasy" in Islam can in some places merit the death penalty. "Truth" must be obeyed. One writer puts it this way:

A core distinction should be drawn between the Qur'an, which does not prescribe a punishment for apostasy in this life (only in the life to come) and traditional Islamic jurisprudence – texts such as the Hadith and Sunna – which mandate the death penalty for a sane male apostate, and lifelong imprisonment for a woman in a similar position.[11]

Those teachings can be invoked to justify harsh treatment for those who try to leave the Muslim faith. As Islam becomes more militant in many countries, members of minority religions have reason to be afraid, particularly if their family roots are in Islam.

Faced with such intolerance in different religions, both in past centuries and in the present day, many consider the fault to lie in the nature

---

10 See Roger Trigg, *Reality at Risk: A Defence of Realism in Philosophy and the Sciences*, 2nd ed., Harvester Wheatsheaf (Simon & Schuster), Hemel Hempstead, 1980, p. 29 ff.

11 Rupert Shortt: *Christianophobia: A Faith Under Attack*, Random House, London, 2012, p. 78.

of religion. It is of its nature, we are told, absolutist. What is precisely meant by absolutism is sometimes unclear. It is usually seen as a bad thing, but what is precisely wrong can be left worryingly vague. Is it the mere claim of objective truth, the idea that one has exclusive access to it, or the attempt to obtain the acknowledgment of such truth by others? Is it perhaps the view that any means justifies that end, so that it does not matter if the acknowledgment is freely given or forcibly obtained through all means of coercion available, including torture and threats of death?

Each of these is sometimes identified with absolutism. Certainly, if I cannot claim that the truth I believe in also applies to you, I may have no reason to make you believe, too. Relativism once again seems the tolerant option. Yet the notion of an objective truth should carry with it the idea of a shared rationality. We can have reasons for accepting or rejecting alleged truths. Relativism cannot claim that, but simply holds that our way of life is ours. What does that say about our attitude toward those with different sets of beliefs, or in different forms of life? We have no need to believe we ought to be tolerant, or even indifferent toward them. We may just want to force others to be like us. The fact that truth has been abstracted from the picture can be just as dangerous as keeping it in. There can then, in principle, be no reason for tolerance or forbearance, given that all basis for rationality has been removed.

The urge to make others see the truth can be a motive for violence, oppression, and other forms of coercion, but much violence in history has been committed just as an exercise of power over others. I need not think I am right, in some objective sense, or be pursuing some truth, to want to bend others to my will. Ruthlessness does not have to be cloaked in self-righteousness. Sometimes it can be just ruthless. Similarly, whole societies can pursue policies of expansion, oppression, and even enslavement through a simple exercise of self-interested power. An ideology may help, but coercion is not the sole preserve of those who want to spread truth.

William Cavanaugh claims that there is no reason "to suppose that so-called secular ideologies such as nationalism, patriotism, capitalism, Marxism and liberalism are any less prone to be absolutist, divisive and irrational than belief in, for example, the biblical God." Yet he faces the objection that there is a difference in that, for religious believers, "the object of their beliefs is claimed to be absolute." This is somehow associated with the idea of transcendence. Cavanaugh explains that, according to this view, "it is this absolutism that makes obedience blind and causes the believer to subjugate all means to a transcendent end."[12]

Yet again, it is unclear what is meant by absolute in this connection. There may be an implied reference to the omnipotence of God. The relevance of that to justifying every means to a desired end remains far from clear. If God is understood to have endowed humans with rationality, and the freedom with which to use it, it could be part of the divine will that we all respect that freedom, and also use our own reason rather than brute force. The idea that the end justifies the means does not respect the intrinsic God-endowed worth and dignity of each human being. Revolutionary Marxism was quite happy to sacrifice whole economic classes for the greater good. Christianity, on the other hand, has normally insisted that because each human is precious in the sight of God, humans cannot be used as pawns in a wider game. In that respect, Kant's famous dictum in moral philosophy that one should treat others only as ends and not means comes from a basic Christian understanding.

Cavanaugh's own test of absolutism is that it comes down to "that for which one is willing to kill."[13] Yet a complication is that religion can often inspire pacifism, itself a so-called absolutist view about the invariant value of human life, to which there are no exceptions. Similarly, a view of the inherent dignity of humans on the grounds that all are made in the image of God might produce the view that torture and other such means of coercion were themselves absolutely wrong, and never justified. Cavanaugh pointedly asks how many Americans would be willing to kill for their Christian faith, in comparison with those who would be willing to kill for their country. His conclusion is that the nation-state is likely to produce more "absolutist fervor" than religion. Another conclusion, however, might be that "absolutist" is a term used in so many different ways that it has become little more than a word of abuse.

---

12 William Cavanaugh, *The Myth of Religious Violence*, Oxford University Press, New York, 2009, p. 55.
13 Cavanaugh, *The Myth of Religious Violence*, p. 56.

HUMAN FREEDOM

Some may feel that religion produces particular dangers, even if it does not have a monopoly on oppression. The Inquisition was seen as evidence of a more general authoritarianism by the Roman Catholic Church, intent on preserving its own power at all costs. Putting the issue like that immediately takes us away from the issue of truth into an altogether different realm, one in which the Church would have to stand accused according to its own principles. It claims to be purveying Christian truth, not participating in a human power struggle. The Church's association with oppression created a poisonous legacy that is still hard to eradicate. Even at the end of the seventeenth century, John Locke was aware of the sufferings of many under the Inquisition. In his advocacy of "toleration," it is striking that Locke's tolerance does not extend to papists. He writes tersely in an early work that "papists are not to enjoy the benefit of toleration, because, where they have power, they think themselves bound to deny it to others." He also refers to the "cruelty" of their principles and practices.[14]

In fact, as we are told, "the Inquisition became a major analytical tool in the condemnation of all forms of religious persecution."[15] In Protestant countries, this could take the form, as in the case of Locke, of a principled theological protest. In his famous "Letter Concerning Toleration," he wrote:

Faith is not faith without believing. Whatever profession we make, to whatever outward worship we conform, if we are not fully satisfied in our own mind that the one is true, and the other well-pleasing unto God, such profession and such practice, far from being any furtherance, are indeed great obstacles to salvation.[16]

The Inquisition was, even its own terms, doomed to failure because although it could coerce people into outward conformity, it could not guarantee a true change of heart and an alteration of sincere belief.

14 John Locke, "An Essay on Toleration" (1667), in *Political Essays*, ed. Mark Goldie, Cambridge University Press, Cambridge, 1997, p. 152.
15 Bethencourt, *The Inquisition*, p. 10.
16 John Locke, "A Letter Concerning Toleration," in *Two Treatises of Government and A Letter Concerning Toleration*, ed. Ian Shapiro, Yale University Press, New Haven, CT, 2003, p. 219.

Yet the Church was presumably attempting to produce a repentance that was genuine when judged by the God it was supposedly serving. It had a political effect beyond Europe. Toward the end of the eighteenth century, when the Inquisition was under attack but still functioning in many countries, Thomas Jefferson proclaimed that "Truth can stand by itself." He continued by saying: "Subject opinion to coercion: whom will you make your inquisitors? Fallible men; men governed by bad passions, by private as well as public reasons."[17] James Madison similarly had the Inquisition in mind in his influential "Memorial and Remonstrance," concerning the proposed public funding of religion in postcolonial Virginia. Arguing that it was a form of continued establishment of religion, he saw it as an infringement on basic religious liberty by government, saying that "distant as it may be in its present form, from the Inquisition, it differs from it only in degree." He saw the one as the first step and the latter as the last in "the career of intolerance."[18]

The problem with forms of coercion, such as the Inquisition, is not simply that they claim grounding in objective truth. Locke was claiming objective truth for his belief that God wants the free response of humans, not a forced and insincere outward show. Something else is going wrong. Might it be the claiming of certainty by the Inquisitors, a certainty that excludes all other views? Jefferson's reference to human fallibility is not misplaced. What right has anyone to be so certain of their position that they can force their views on others who disagree? The issue then is not so much whether there is a truth all should equally accept. It is how we can be sure we know what it is.

If we regard human freedom as God-given, along with our rationality, we have a powerful argument for accepting its exercise, even when we disapprove of the way others use their freedom. This insight is at the root of democracy. For Locke, we are "born free, as we are born rational."[19] If God has given us such freedom, it seems to follow that it should be respected, even in situations where some might be tempted to think they are serving God through restricting the freedom of others. As Locke observes, in a sentiment we have seen later taken up by Thomas

17 Thomas Jefferson, "Notes on the State of Virginia," in *The Separation of Church and State: Writings on a Fundamental American Freedom by America's Founders*, ed. Forrest Church, Beacon Press, Boston, 2004, p. 53.

18 James Madison, "Memorial and Remonstrance," in Church, p. 67.

19 John Locke, "Second Treatise," in *Two Treatises*, ed. Shapiro, p. 125.

Jefferson: "Truth certainly would do well enough, if she were left to shift for herself." He continues: "If truth makes not her way into the understanding by her own light, she will be but the weaker for any borrowed force violence can add to her."[20] For Locke, however, toleration could only go so far. He was not willing to extend it to atheists, on the grounds that they would not feel themselves bound by promises or obligations. He was also unwilling for the state to tolerate those who "deliver themselves up to the protection and service of another prince," such as the Pope.[21]

These caveats remind us that religious freedom can never itself be total, even if we disagree with Locke's restrictions on it. A democratic state has to defend itself precisely against those who, because of their religious beliefs, may attempt to destroy that state and all it stands for. Modern forms of terrorism may well fall into that category. The defense of freedom demands that we cannot tolerate those who do not, in their actions, respect such freedom. Individual freedom, even when we can disagree with the uses to which it is put, must be respected and protected. The reasons for that are historically deeply rooted in a Christian view of the world of the kind Locke expressed. God, it was held, has given us free will, and the rationality with which to guide our freedom. Compelled and insincere belief is worth nothing compared with a sincere commitment to God, freely offered.

The idea of human freedom can be understood as itself an important element of what is objectively true. We would not otherwise be able to come to any rational understanding of what is true. Coerced and compelled beliefs can be just as likely to be false as true, as it all depends on the source of the compulsion. The Inquisitors believed that they were in full possession of what was true, as they were acting in the name of a Church that could claim to carry with it the authority of God. Yet they failed to understand that unless people take on the responsibility for judging truth for themselves, their apparent commitment becomes worthless.

Human freedom is integral to a general truth of the human condition. One can try by argument and reasoning to draw others into what one sees as truth. One can proclaim and preach it. That is far from

20 Locke, "A Letter Concerning Toleration," p. 241.
21 Locke, *Two Treatises*, p. 245.

compulsion, and rejection is both possible and often likely. Further, if God wants only a free response and the exercise of human free will, there is a theological reason, even within Christianity, for a plurality of beliefs. Not everyone, for good or bad reasons, will come to the same conclusions. The existence of religious diversity may not be itself just a consequence of human freedom and the exercise of choice, but a pre-condition for its proper exercise. Our choices cannot be free if we have no alternatives from which to choose.

The Inquisition seemed to many Christians to be wrong at the deepest theological level. The idea of imposing Christian truth seemed to be at odds with its content. This sad historical episode was not just an example of religious dogmatism, but an example of one group of people trying to enforce conformity on another. This is not a characteristic peculiar to religion, or the result of religious diversity, but remains a constant temptation to humans.

There is the omnipresent desire to use force so as to bend people to our will. Sometimes we simply dislike the strange, or are fearful of "the other." We can be cocooned in our own society and easily use violence against those outside of it. Humans often feel threatened in some way by difference and distinctiveness. Jews have often faced that kind of situation in many societies. An old cartoon in the British satirical magazine *Punch* of 1854 illustrates this simple human trait well.[22] Two ordinary workmen see a particularly well-dressed man passing. One says to the other, "Who's 'im, Bill?" With the answer given, "A stranger!" the first one promptly says, "'Eave 'arf a brick at 'im!"

There is also the danger of being so certain of our own position that we consider that any who disagree are not merely in error but are culpably so. If truth seems so transparent, it is easy to assume that those who do not find it so are either fools or knaves. Either way, they appear to deserve correction. Many are suspicious of those who have this kind of certainty. It is crucial to see that one's view of the truth is not infallible. Any claim to truth about reality has to carry with it an element of risk if truth is not the mere shadow cast by our beliefs. None of us is omniscient, although we all run the risk of deceiving ourselves into thinking that we are.

22 *A Century of Punch*, ed. R. E. Williams, William Heinemann, London, 1956, p. 248.

TRUTH AND COERCION

THE THREAT OF "FUNDAMENTALISM"

In religion, the specter of so-called fundamentalism is often raised. How it is defined is a moot point. It could mean a mere insistence on the truth of certain core features of a faith, and an unwillingness to compromise. Sometimes there may appear an aggressive dogmatism that appears to ride roughshod over alternatives. It can seem to be an unattractive insistence on certain "truths," stemming from fear to meet challenges in a calm and open way, or even to listen to them. For this reason, it sometimes seems as if fundamentalism is just a synonym for bigots and those who embody intolerance of others. At worst, it can be a word that just describes those with whom we disagree, because they insist on what they claim is truth.

Sometimes the word is used in a more restricted way to refer to the way in which people rely on the words of texts in a book like the Bible or the Qur'an, and regard them, even when torn out of context, as the direct word of God that has to be taken literally and obeyed. As Richard Dawkins puts it, in that case, "the truth of the holy book [is taken] as an axiom, not the end product of a process of reasoning." He comments that fundamentalists assume that "the book is true, and if the evidence seems to contradict it, it is the evidence that must be thrown out, not the book."[23] It is the difference, in the context of the Christian faith, between saying that something is true because it is in the Bible and holding that it is the Bible because it is true. In the latter case, reasons for its truth, be they historical or otherwise, may be adduced to support what is said and to convince others. A mere appeal to the Bible could appear to be the question at issue. The origin of the term "fundamentalist" at the beginning of the twentieth century lay in a strict adherence to the truth of the Bible, as setting out the "fundamentals" of the Christian faith. It sprang up particularly in the United States in the context of modern biblical criticism coming from Germany, and a perceived "liberalism" in theology that wanted to revise basic doctrine.

"Modernists" wanted to make Christian theology acceptable to modern assumptions that queried, for example, the compatibility of miracles with science. The growth of science provided alternative standards of

23 Richard Dawkins, *The God Delusion*, Bantam Press, London, 2006, p. 282.

what it was to be rational, which made faith appear precarious when it insisted on transcendent realities. Fundamentalism can appear to be a frightened reaction to such challenges. Instead of using reason to try to expose the limitations of such views, fundamentalists leave reason to the self-appointed atheist "rationalists" and retreat to an insistence on the inerrancy of Scripture.

According to such fundamentalism, God's character is unshakeable, and so must be the revelation of His Word. If God is "the absolute," He must have revealed Himself absolutely. It is a quest for certainty in a world that seems ever more uncertain of everything. It is a desire to be so sure of what we are committed to that we are not tempted to falter. Compromise looks like a denial of truth, and so "no compromise" becomes a fundamentalist slogan. In the Christian context, although fundamentalists have a lively sense of evil and sin at work in the world, their demand for certainty can exclude any admission that they themselves may be caught up in that same web of sin and fallibility, and need to adopt some humility. That would presumably allow the seeds of doubt to be sown.

This dogmatic certainty, as an attitude founded in religion, spills over into politics in many places, with unpredictable results. It is the antithesis of a democratic attitude, but fundamentalists often feel threatened by modern Western society, which seems to have doubt built into its core. This applies not just to Christian fundamentalists; it is a significant feature of the last generation that fundamentalisms of various kinds have simultaneously grown in influence in different religions and different continents.

Forms of Islamic fundamentalism, with a characteristic mixture of certainty and intolerance, are well known. At their extreme, they give rise to acts of terrorism. Yet all the main religions now seem to have "fundamentalist" wings. Judaism, both within Israel and in the wider diaspora, has the ultra-Orthodox, who are gaining in numbers and influence. Forms of Hinduism in India have become more sharp-edged and nationalistic. Buddhism in Sri Lanka has exposed a militant side. The retreat to dogmatism and confrontation with others may everywhere betray the same basic insecurity and fear of modern trends. In each case, traditions have become conscious of major challenges. Once a tradition becomes self-conscious in that way, intolerance toward others, together with a deliberate dogmatism, becomes a possible defensive reaction.

Fundamentalism can strive for a distinct identity that marks its adherents off from others. The attitude helps its adherents, of whatever religion, confront the pervasive sense of uncertainty in a fast-changing world, and provides a shared sense of identity and belonging. They want to differentiate themselves from the wider society they despise, sometimes in dress, but mainly belief and behavior. This can produce a more inward-looking community, with closely knit family units and a higher birthrate than in the outside world. Yet they are usually embedded within a larger religion, and their influence on it can be disproportionate to their numbers. A highly organized and determined minority can always galvanize a less organized, and perhaps less committed, majority.

Fundamentalists seem to want the logical certainty of mathematics for religious faith. Knowledge has implied the right to be sure, but even knowledge does not imply certainty. I can know without knowing that I know, as a hesitant, but correct, answer in a quiz might illustrate. Conversely, certainty itself does not entail knowledge. The world is full of people who are certain of many things and yet are plain wrong. Certainty and truth are not invariable bedfellows. In the world of religion, where ideas of the transcendent come into play, honest doubt has a role.

Fundamentalists are seen to insist on truth to the exclusion of any possibility of dialogue. They can make it look as if any attempt to claim objective truth must arrogantly rule out other possibilities. Their assertion of truth appears to coerce. Many react by wanting to denounce all such exclusivism with regard to truth. The issue, however, is not the danger of claiming any truth, but the lack of humility of those who exhibit certainty about what is true.

Truth may itself be coercive in a benign sense. We can be led to it, not forced to accept it. This was presumably what Locke, and then Jefferson, meant when they held that truth could look after itself. If we are rational, we ought to be able to recognize what is true when faced with it. Truth concerns what is the case, and when we are operating within language, this means that the sentences that we speak, and the propositions expressed in them, claim truth. They are true by virtue of the nature of something beyond themselves. According to some philosophic views, such as those we have examined derived from the later

Wittgenstein, cleaving to such propositions, pulled out of their social context, itself constitutes an irrational fundamentalism. The truth of propositions cannot then hold outside of the surroundings that give them meaning.

This is to confuse fundamentalism with a metaphysical foundation-alism that demands that our beliefs are ontologically grounded. God must exist (in a realist sense) if our beliefs in God are to be justifiable. It is this sense that D. Z. Phillips invokes when he pithily says that "real-ists are foundationalists, for whom beliefs never yield certainty." In that way, they are certainly distinct from fundamentalists. Phillips goes on to see this as a weakness, however, and to criticize some philosophers for not capturing the language of faith, and the certainty he, follow-ing Wittgenstein, thinks is bound up with it. He says: "They cannot capture the conviction involved in a confession of faith. Penelhum and Trigg, along with other foundationalists, turn the conviction into mere probability."[24]

In other words, realism involves a tentative belief that is not the mark of true religious faith. The ironic point is that this stress on certainty can make all religious faith look like that of the fundamentalist. It becomes a dogmatic certainty impervious to reason. The word "foundationalist" might even then imply a connection between the realist stress on truth and a more general "fundamentalism." This seems to be envisaged even by Rowan Williams, when he distances himself from the idea that "reli-gious commitment is seen first as the acceptance of propositions which determine acceptable behavior." He then immediately says that this is "the kind of religiousness we tend now to call fundamentalist." We can-not, he says, preempt religious meanings "by requiring instant assent to descriptions of reality offered by straightforward revelation."[25]

Williams may be merely emphasizing the inevitable role of interpre-tation. Texts, and even revelations, do not come already interpreted, and fundamentalists tend not to take that point seriously. Reference to Wittgenstein's later theory of meaning in the same paragraph suggests, however, the influence of the view that meaning is determined by con-text in his understanding of what it is to claim truth. Many philosophers

24 D. Z. Phillips, "On Really Believing," *Is God Real?*, ed. Joseph Runzo, Macmillan, Basingstoke, 1993, p. 105.
25 Williams, p. 16.

and theologians of a pluralist disposition are certainly ready to make the jump from seeing a claim to truth put forward as a justification for a commitment, and condemning it as fundamentalist. Even claiming truth on one's own part can seem arrogant. Appeals to objective truth are seen as a coercive way of manipulating others.

Accepting this means that we remove the possibility of using reason as the route to truth. The alternative to reason is the deliberate use of power, and arbitrary authority. We are then faced with a coercion that has to be revealed as such, and truth drops out of sight as irrelevant. When horrors are inflicted in the name of truth, what is wrong is not that truth is invoked, but that human beings should not be treated in that way. Their freedom and rationality should be respected. This is what appeals to human dignity are about. It is a sadness of human history, and indeed of life today, that evils can be inflicted in the name of the very religions that also uphold the intrinsic importance of what it is to be human. Certainty about truth can lead to actions that clearly contradict the truth of the beliefs that inspired them.

8

RELIGIOUS DIVERSITY AND IDENTITY

SOURCES OF AUTHORITY

In the previous chapter, I showed that many can feel threatened by the diversity and rapid change of modern life, even in the sphere of religious belief. Fundamentalism is one reaction to this. Paradoxically, philosophical relativism can also insulate us collectively from others by removing the possibility that there is anything to learn from them. Whatever we, and the group we belong to, believe is true for us. One sociologist comments that "when religious differences are strongly embedded in ethnic identities, the cognitive threat of the ideas of others is relatively weak."[1] Challenges to those beliefs from outside our own society, however defined, do not point us to a wider truth. We are more concerned with who we are than with the justification of the beliefs that help to define us and our way of life. The idea of a universal truth applying to all can be ignored, and could destabilize our society by possibly undermining the beliefs that help define it. The more objective truth is decried, the more likely it is for a premium to be placed on social cohesion. The more identity is valued, the more likely it is for concerns about truth to seem irrelevant.

The maintenance of a common identity can easily become the priority. Even if groups we think they possess important truths, their maintenance and transmission, and the preservation of the community in which they are held, can progressively appear ever more important.

---

1 Steve Bruce, "The Social Process of Secularization," in *Blackwell Companion to Sociology of Religion*, ed. Richard K. Fenn, Blackwell, Oxford, 2001, p. 260.

Issues concerning authority often loom large in religious disputes. Who has the authority to define, and to safeguard, what is supposed to be true? Saying that the authority resides in a holy text such as the Bible or the Qur'an transfers the question to who can be trusted to give the correct, or approved, interpretation of the text. Schools of interpretation can grow up, and disputes arise about who the experts are who can be trusted.

In the case of Christianity, the Roman Catholic Church, with its acknowledged hierarchy, jealously guarded the right to interpret scripture and for a long time was reluctant to allow its translation into vernacular languages so that everyone could read and decide its meaning for themselves. For some, the more extreme features of the Protestant Reformation confirmed these fears. Many drew their own conclusions from the Bible, taking little notice of the tradition of the Church, and felt free to set up new Christian communities. An enforced cohesion gave way to a seemingly anarchic freedom. Although freedom unconstrained by truth could prove dangerous, that did not solve the question of who should define truth, or, at least, what is to be believed.

Because religious beliefs are so deeply rooted in human nature, they are important to those who wield power, who see them as a threat. Such beliefs pose a separate source of authority beyond, and perhaps in competition with, the state, undermining its cohesion. Political leaders often want to use the moral force of religion and its motivating power to their own ends. It is a typical act of totalitarians to attempt even to stamp out religion, because it poses a potentially uncontrollable threat to their authority. Either way, it is important for them either to control religion for their own ends or to suppress it. They cannot allow it to retain any form of independent authority lest it become a focus for dissent. The demise of Communism in Eastern Europe in the late twentieth century illustrated how fruitless an effort this was. The cognitive science of religion predicts that impulses leading to religion will always be present in humans, and religion is always likely to be resurgent in one form or another. The sociological theory of an inevitable secularization and the marginalizing of all religion that arose in the 1960s was always doomed as a theory. Pockets of greater secularization, as in Western Europe at the beginning of the twenty-first century, are always liable to be the exception from a global point of view.

Rulers and political leaders can find it useful for the power of their regimes to be underpinned by the implied approval not just of the church or other religious institution but even of God. The doctrine of the "divine right of kings" was used in the seventeenth century to validate monarchical power. Divine authority then becomes transferred to earthly power, in ways that have often been mirrored in modern times when totalitarian rulers have ascribed godlike qualities to themselves. Religious identity and national loyalty are then combined and help express an identity that minorities in those nations may find uncomfortable. There is a perennial tug-of-war between two understandings of power by those who attempt to use it One is that sacred authority, in particular that of the one God, however mediated, is separate from, is superior to, and judges that of the state. The other is that the state is the ultimate source of authority, perhaps using the power of religion to forge a loyalty to itself.

The first view is symbolized by the cross surmounting a crown, or, more explicitly, by the words of the service for the Coronation of a British monarch. In 1953, for example, Queen Elizabeth II promised in Westminster Abbey "to maintain the Laws of God and the true profession of the Gospel." However, the danger has always been that temporal authority, whether it was trying conscientiously to uphold what it saw as truth – perhaps in cooperation with the church, – or using religion cynically, would supersede spiritual authority. The history of Europe is replete with examples of battles between state and church. The issue of the church as an institution free from external political control was a constant problem both for Catholic and Protestant states. Conversely, the dominance of one religious institution could provide problems for dissenting minorities.

Divisions within a religion, or between religions, can assume such importance in the hearts and minds of believers that the stability of the state can be threatened. Political and religious concerns can often be bound up with each other. In contemporary Northern Ireland, for example, it is remarkably easy for commentators to switch from describing "loyalists" and "republicans" to talking of "Protestants" and "Catholics." The terms are not synonymous, and there is no contradiction in being a Catholic Unionist. Even so, religious and the political terms can each generally map onto the same communities in a divided society, and religious divisions can fuel antagonisms.

FREEDOM FOR INSTITUTIONS

Even if religious affiliations can seem a source of trouble, institutional freedom for organizations existing at a level between the individual and the state is crucial, because they provide important buffers between the individual and the state. As the U.S. Supreme Court Justice Samuel Alito put it in an important opinion about the religious freedom of churches to appoint their own ministers, "throughout our Nation's history, religious bodies have been the preeminent example of private associations that have 'acted as critical buffers between the individual and the power of the State.'"[2] He goes on to comment that "it is easy to forget that the autonomy of religious groups, both here in the United States and abroad, has often served as a shield against oppressive laws." He argues that the religion clauses in the First Amendment to the U.S. Constitution (about nonestablishment of religion and its free exercise) "protect a private sphere within which religious bodies are free to govern themselves in accordance with their own beliefs."

Even in a liberal society, the less individuals live by the discipline of various religious institutions, the more powerful the state has to become. It has to fill the vacuum created by a loss of other forms of authority, particularly moral authority, and may have to introduce increasingly burdensome regulation. This is particularly noticeable in a democratic society, but the need for any church to be free of the direction of the state if it is to pursue its own mission has always been present. The first article of Magna Carta, signed by King John in a meadow on the banks of the Thames in 1215, concerned the freedom of the English Church (the *Ecclesia Anglicana*). It is one of the few articles of the charter still in force in English law.

Religious freedom demands not just one but a diversity of institutions that can nurture different points of view. However, the demands of social cohesion highlight the dangers of this, stressing the importance of a common loyalty and shared standards. Religious diversity can be seen as the expression of a free society, but also as an obstacle to the possibility of enough shared values to enable everyone to cooperate. The

2 *Hosanna-Tabor Evangelical Lutheran Church and School v. Employment Opportunity Commission*, 132 S. Ct. 694, 712 (2012) (Alito J. concurring).

idea of one ultimate truth, binding everyone together with common beliefs, makes a continuous competition between rival views, or rival institutions, appear very threatening.

King John offered freedom to the English Church, not to all religious institutions. Religious diversity was not then an option. The relation of the church with temporal authority, in the shape of the monarch, was a side issue to the question of national identity. The church could be a powerful focus for that because it had no competitor. Things changed with the Reformation, however, and before long the Church of England faced challenges from two wings. Some tried to maintain their traditional Roman Catholicism, while radical Protestants used their study of the Bible, now translated into English, to come to radical conclusions of their own.

The threat to national stability became all too obvious. The Gunpowder Plot of 1605, still remembered on November 5, narrowly failed to blow up the Houses of Parliament on the occasion of the State Opening of Parliament. The plot had been orchestrated by influential Catholic families, and Roman Catholics were regarded as being in league with Catholic countries. The Armada from Catholic Spain had threatened England in 1588. On the other hand, Puritans and others demanded a greater religious freedom that then threatened to dissolve the bonds that kept citizens together. In the next generation, England would be torn apart by a civil war in which religious factors were all too prominent. Different ideas of church government and opposition to Anglican bishops played their part, producing the growth of "dissent" and "nonconformity," both words suggesting a breakdown in uniformity and the dissolving of social bonds.

In this unstable situation, with cracks appearing in the social edifice, the first modern argument for individual religious freedom was made. In 1612, Thomas Helwys, who founded the first Baptist Church in England that year, wrote a treatise upholding the idea of religious liberty.[3] He rather unwisely sent a personal copy to King James I in which he inscribed on the flyleaf the view that "if the King has authority to make spiritual lords and laws, then he is an immortal God and not a mortal

---

3 Thomas Helwys, *A Short Declaration of the Mystery of Iniquity*, ed. R. Groves, Mercer University Press, Macon, GA, 1998.

man."[4] The king was not impressed, and Helwys ended his days in Newgate Prison in London.

Helwys drew a distinction that reflected Protestant thinking: between an earthly kingdom subject to the king and a heavenly kingdom over which the king could have no jurisdiction. Helwys proclaims: "Let it suffice the King to have all rule over the people's bodies and goods, and let not our lord the King give his power to be exercised over the spirits of his people."[5] "Men's religion," Helwys says, "is between God and themselves."

Helwys's arguments for individual religious freedom are profoundly theological. He asks: "Is it not most equal that men should choose their religion themselves, seeing they only must stand themselves before the judgement seat of God to answer for themselves, when it shall be no excuse for them to say we were commanded or compelled to be of this religion by the king or by them that had authority from him?"[6] The stress on the importance to God of inward belief and not just outward conformity would be taken up later in the seventeenth century by John Locke.

This thesis of the two kingdoms lives on in many human rights charters, such as the European Convention on Human Rights. A right to inner freedom of belief is regarded as absolute, but when it comes to expressing or "manifesting" that belief in public, it becomes highly qualified, subject to the protection of "the rights and freedoms of others." It is questionable, however, whether any religion can be split in this way between personal, private belief and public behavior, so that one is sacrosanct but the other is subject to the control of the state. The assertion of the priority of religious duties to God above the demands of secular authority has been transmuted into the distinction between a private, spiritual realm of religion and a public, secular one. Some Protestant sects have succumbed to the temptation of such "quietism" and even opted out of any contribution to the public good, at the extreme separating themselves, as the North American Amish have, from wider society. The tug-of-war between religious belief and the competing demands of a sometimes hostile society can seem too wearing.

---

4 Helwys, *A Short Declaration*, p. xxiv.
5 Helwys, *A Short Declaration*, p. 45.
6 Helwys, *A Short Declaration*, p. 37.

At one extreme is a society where religious conformity is enforced, and at the other is one that splinters into different communities that try to keep away from each other. Helwys's own views, however inspiring, are themselves a warning. He was an important witness to the role of individual religious freedom. With his stress on the individual's responsibility before God, he was very suspicious of any ecclesiastical authority. The Roman Catholic Church and Anglican bishops were both fair game. He turned his fire also on other groups who were beginning to come together. He was an early Baptist, but other Puritans and Separatists were beginning to emerge, in disputes, particularly about church governance, that would produce separate Christian denominations, such as the Presbyterians and Congregationalists. He opposed them all, and he fell out with some of his fellow Baptists as well. In overheated prose, he denounced all and sundry, even those who were apparently close to him theologically, as "false prophets" and "infidels,"[7] terms that even today can be used to fan the flames of religious intolerance.

This ferment stemmed from a focus on the role of the individual conscience. The notion of truth looms large in that Helwys is quite clear about the false beliefs of his opponents, but a truth defined in terms of the e conscience of each individual is immensely destabilizing. Some can be sure they alone are right and everyone else is wrong and, as the English Civil War demonstrated, can often be prepared to resort to violence to prove their point. For Helwys, the individual conscience is supreme, regardless of what others think. This guidance by an "inner light," a notion that was criticized by Locke, can degenerate into a corrosive subjectivism. If I imagine that I possess truth and no one else does, and if others who disagree with me take a similar line, objective truth drops out of the picture as irrelevant. What I think is right, and if you cannot see that, you are wicked, an "infidel." Disagreement can be healthy, but if those disagreeing merely denounce each other and walk away, the result can be devastating.

The result of the ferment exhibited in the writings of Thomas Helwys showed the dangers of religious diversity and, by extension, the religious freedom he advocated. There was a major splintering of Protestantism,

---

7 See his attack on "Brownists," who themselves advocated separation from the Church of England, *Short Declaration*, p. 91.

with the Church of England spawning such major worldwide Christian denominations as the Presbyterians, Congregationalists, and Baptists, not to mention other groups such as the Quakers. There were major political repercussions, and these religious tensions were a spur to the "Pilgrim Fathers" who left England and founded Massachusetts. Division and discord provide no argument against religious freedom, which lies at the heart of all democracy, but such precedents indicate why religious diversity and religious freedom were feared by many then and still are today. Many feel threatened by difference and can react violently.

AN "INNER LIGHT?"

Those who went to Massachusetts were inspired to set up their own version of a godly society, based on Congregationalist principles. Popular American mythology holds that they crossed the ocean in search of religious liberty, and it is true in that they collectively wanted to be free from the authority of the Church of England and its bishops. That did not mean, however, that they were eager for their colony to be populated by others who disagreed with them. They wanted freedom for themselves, and those who were like-minded, to live as they collectively chose. They literally had no room for those who disagreed. Issues of identity, both religious and civil, loomed large. They would not tolerate what they saw as blasphemy, corruption, and error. Massachusetts proscribed and banished Anglicans, Baptists, and any "individual who dared challenge its theology, moral code, or political dominion."[8] Notoriously, it even hanged Quakers, who were regarded as a particular menace, including Mary Dyer, now commemorated on Boston Common.

One person expelled from Massachusetts was Roger Williams. He is admired by many as one of the first champions of religious freedom, and the philosopher Martha Nussbaum describes him as one of the seventeenth century's "great apostles of religious liberty."[9] As she points out, he was willing to extend religious liberty to all, even atheists.[10] His

---

8 John Barry, *Roger Williams and the Creation of the American Soul*, Viking, New York, 2012, p. 374.
9 Martha Nussbaum, *Liberty of Conscience*, Basic Books, New York, 2008, p. 36.
10 Martha Nussbaum, *The New Religious Intolerance*, Harvard University Press, Cambridge, MA, 2012, p. 74.

major work was written in London in 1644 and called *The Bloudy Tenent of Persecution*. Roger Williams was certainly ready to accept radical religious difference. However, his own life, like that of Thomas Helwys, illustrates the problems that can arise through the passionate espousing of liberty above all else. An exile from Anglican England, he also became an exile from Congregationalist Massachusetts. He then founded the colony of Rhode Island, championing an individualism that ensured that Providence, the town he founded, did not even have a meetinghouse for half a century.[11]

Williams had been influenced by ideas represented in the work of Helwys, which later gained greater currency. He had been living as a boy in London near Newgate when Helwys was imprisoned there, and in Providence later joined a group of Baptists, even being rebaptized.[12] Even so, any form of conformity to a wider community was difficult for him. As John Barry puts it, "conformity is a function of the desire for certainty,"[13] and Williams "had a remarkable willingness to live with doubt and uncertainty." As a result he came to see that "his own worship must be personal and individual, and not communal."[14] It is, of course, also true that an exaggerated sense of personal certainty can also produce radical nonconformity and an unwillingness to cooperate with others, if a person regards everyone else as wrong.

Here lies a deep problem. The more that the individual is made an arbiter of truth, the greater the freedom that person appears to have. The more external standards of truth have to be adhered to, the more questions of authority and power seem to come into the picture, in ways that may distort one's vision of the truth. If I decide what I am to count as true in a stronger sense than just accepting what others preach, my liberty seems untrammeled, but in the religious context, it becomes very likely that I shall find myself in a church with one member. The more I am willing to join in community with others, the more I have to accept common standards of truth. If I then find myself doubting their validity, conformity and sincere commitment may come to be at odds with each other.

---

11 Barry, *Roger Williams*, p. 346.
12 Barry, p. 263.
13 Barry, p. 344.
14 Barry, p. 345.

Truth may have its own intrinsic power of attraction, but once I become unworried when my judgments differ from those of most others, the morass of subjectivism beckons. Reason is shared, and it should give similar answers to different people facing the same questions. A passionate concern for truth can be divisive if pursued to logical extremes without regard for the judgment of others. The idea of orthodoxy can seem an assault on the religious freedom of the individual and an illegitimate constraint on the individual conscience. Championing such an extreme liberty produces a society near breakdown because of the lack of any common principles. In its early days Rhode Island struggled to avoid anarchy and disorder and was notorious in the other colonies.

The views of early Baptists and other radicals, such as Helwys in England and Williams in the American colonies, presaged not just a championing of the idea of religious freedom but an emphasis on the accountability of each individual to God. John Locke was influenced by these ideas, but in his case the influence of the early Enlightenment also showed itself. For Locke, reason was "the candle of the Lord set up by himself in men's minds, which it is impossible for the breath or power of man wholly to distinguish."[15] It was not, as in the later Enlightenment, a secular stick with which to beat religious faith. It was an ally of faith, not its enemy.

The stress on reason was derived from the thinking of the Cambridge Platonists, and reason as "the candle of the Lord" was one of their favorite slogans.[16] It was particularly associated with Benjamin Whichcote, whose sermons John Locke attended at his London church, St. Lawrence Jewry. The Cambridge Platonists were a group of theologians and philosophers much affected by the upheavals of the English Civil War and the irrational animosities it unleashed. They were well aware of the extreme religious subjectivism apparently espoused by some and saw that reason was a common currency all could share. Several of their number were founding members of the Royal Society, the organization for the advancement of science set up after the Restoration of Charles II as king. They considered that truth had to have a

---

15 *Essay Concerning Human Understanding*, 4.3.20, ed. and abr. A. S. Pringle-Pattison, Oxford University Press, Oxford, 1924, p. 280.
16 See Charles Taliaferro and Alison Teply, eds., *Cambridge Platonist Spirituality*, Paulist Press, New York, 2004.

public aspect, although not necessarily limited to what is empirically accessible.

An "inner light" of revelation, or whatever illumination might be appealed to, could not be valid for only one individual. It gave access to an objective truth open to all. Division into separate churches would seem a contradiction of this, and the Cambridge Platonists – and John Locke himself – were associated with what was called "latitudinarianism," the desire that the Church of England should be, within limits, comprehensive, containing as many so-called dissenters as possible. Diversity should be contained within it, not driven out, as long as it concerned matters that were ultimately of little importance, such as the vestments a minister (or "priest") wore, such as a white surplice or a black gown, or whether one knelt for prayer.

The problem is how to decide what is not of central importance, so that internal dissent can be tolerated. At what point does a religious organization, such as a Christian church, allow such variety of belief that it begins to lose its identity? There must be membership rules, which suggests that certain beliefs disqualify someone from participation. Otherwise the institution stands for nothing, without any clear message to outsiders. However, once these rules are too stringent, the whole edifice can quickly splinter.

If a church or religious sect claims to represent truth, it must become extremely disturbing to its members if there are direct competitors putting forward an alternative version. Just as the fact of different religions poses a question about the reliability of religious claims, so, within one religion, too much disagreement undermines the presentation of a gospel. Not only is the message blurred but, at least in the case of Christianity, the fact of disagreement can itself appear to contradict some of its content. A Hindu once challenged a Christian by asking: "How can you preach a gospel of peace and reconciliation, when you cannot be reconciled with your fellow Christians?" There can be no satisfactory answer. Christian disunity is a powerful obstacle to the preaching of a truth that Christianity sees as applying to all.

Locke and his associates attempted to answer the problem by claiming that disunity was unwarranted if it was because of unimportant squabbles about inessentials. For Locke, the crucial test was that believers should hold "Jesus to be the Messiah, and have taken him to be their King, with a sincere endeavour after righteousness in obeying his law."[17] There is plenty of room for dispute about what this involves, but Locke was trying to be inclusive and comprehensive rather than exclusive. The object was to narrow the issues on which a firm stand should be taken, so as to reduce division.

This still leaves the question, simmering since the days of the Spanish Inquisition, of just how standards of belief should be enforced. Even the Inquisition only persecuted those who were seen as baptized members of the Church. Uniformity of practice may not be necessary, but divergence of belief must be limited by any religious organization if it is to maintain its identity. Some beliefs have to remain "core," even if others appear as less essential. There has to be some balance between individual freedom and the need for conformity, so as to preserve the integrity of the institution.

I have already mentioned the role of religious institutions, among others, as important buffers between the individual and the state. Self-regulation and self-discipline are encouraged by social norms such as those inculcated by a religious community. Without intermediate institutions, an extreme individualism takes hold, and we are then in the situation envisaged by the seventeenth-century philosopher Thomas Hobbes, who saw the dangers of a war of all against all. Only the state could guard against that, thought Hobbes.[18] An extreme individualism can in the end undermine individual freedom. He was right to the extent that without other forms of social restraint, only the state can impose order through regulation and more direct forms of coercion.

GROUPS AND INDIVIDUALS

Does one's identity become formed, even partially, by the groups one belongs to, or is it simply the result of who one is as an individual? What role, indeed, does the idea of national identity have? These become difficult questions when posed in the modern context of human rights. Such rights are usually seen as the property of individuals. The first clause of article 9 of the European Convention on Human Rights claims: "everyone has the right to freedom of thought, conscience and religion; this

17 John Locke, *The Reasonableness of Christianity* (1695), Thoemmes Press, Bristol, 1997, reprinted from 1794 ed., p. 112.
18 See Roger Trigg, *Ideas of Human Nature*, 2nd ed., Blackwell, Oxford, 1999, chapter 4.

right includes freedom to change his religion or belief, and freedom, either alone or in community with others, and in public or private, to manifest his religion or belief, in worship, teaching, practice and observance." The article echoes article 18 of the United Nations Universal Declaration of Human Rights, although the right to change religion has never been fully accepted by many Muslim nations. They feel their whole identity has to be bound up with their religion and are afraid of religious diversity. The very way religion is equated with "belief" and "thought, conscience and religion" are put together makes it clear that a highly individualist model is being implied. Individuals have beliefs and follow their consciences. It is strained to say that institutions do. The whole weight of the clause is directed at the protection of individual freedom, particularly in the case of the crucial right to change one's religion.

This goes well with the idea of democratic freedoms. Democracies are built up from the decisions of individuals. The majority gets its way. That is why the notion of rights is important in any democracy, since minorities, too, have to be protected. Unless a democratic society degenerates into the dictatorship of the majority, dissenting voices have not only to be heard but even nurtured, paradoxical as it may seem. Democracy thrives on the possibility of alternatives. The concept of democracy assumes disagreement and provides mechanisms to manage it. It is the end of democracy if a majority, by winning a vote and implementing a policy, manages to snuff out different opinions. Different civil institutions existing apart from the state ensure that different visions of the common good are nurtured. They have to be an integral part of democratic society.

Article 9 of the European Convention on Human Rights gives a nod in the direction of institutions by mentioning the possibility of being "in community with others." There is an unresolved tension between the claims of institutions and the rights of individuals. How far can human rights allow for the fostering of group rights, especially when institutions appear to bear down on the freedom of individuals? Some groups may make claims on individuals that appear unacceptable by normal democratic standards. However, unless rules are enforced, any institution or group can lose its identity and purpose. This is true of a golf club, whose members have to accept some common rules and a code of behavior. This is an even more pressing issue for religious institutions that regard themselves as repositories of truths. Without some agreed standards of belief and behavior the distinctiveness of the institution is lost. However, enforcing them may at times appear an assault on the freedom of conscience of its individual members, which itself ought to be an avenue to truth.

In his *Letter Concerning Toleration*, John Locke was particularly concerned with religious freedom in an increasingly pluralist society. He defined a church as "a voluntary society of men, joining themselves together of their own accord."[19] He presumably meant by "men" humans and was not excluding women. Just because a church is a free and voluntary society, he claims that "nobody is born a member of any church; otherwise the religion of parents would descend unto children, by the same right of inheritance as their temporal estates." This is fully in accord with the spirit of human rights documents, implying a freedom of choice that of its nature is likely to produce a pluralist society. Individuals may form different churches or other kinds of institution.

This idea of pluralism and diversity as the concomitant of free individual choice is a constituent of the idea of democracy. A top-down enforcement of conformity to a religion, or a particular brand of religion, inevitably assumes the group has priority over the individual. This contrasts with a view of the individual as the basic unit of any society, with the nature of institutions following the choices of individuals. The latter view does not find favor within Islam, nor has it been a traditional Catholic picture. Locke portrays a characteristically Protestant view of religion, in which individual sincere commitment has to be the spring of all genuine religion.

This still leaves the question as to the nature of the commitment. What beliefs does it include? I can make up my own religion, but there would then be no community of like-minded believers. There must be a body of doctrine or agreed understanding to accept or reject. How is that to be transmitted so that it can be offered as a viable option? There has to be an institution in continuing existence for someone to choose to belong to it or not. A pluralist society with diverse beliefs implies the existence of diverse communities and institutions ready to preach and explain what they believe. Otherwise each generation has to start afresh.

19 *Two Treatises of Government and A Letter Concerning Toleration*, ed. Ian Shapiro, Yale University Press, New Haven, CT, 2003, p. 220.

MUST SOCIAL NORMS BE ENFORCED?

Diversity and democracy go hand in hand. Democracy is a mechanism for dealing with diversity, and the possibility of individual free choice creates the likelihood of disagreement and difference. Religious freedom ensures religious pluralism. At the very least, people must be free to reject the prevailing religious assumptions of a given society. The connection of religious pluralism with democracy is a basic theme of judgments of the European Court of Human Rights. In one major set of cases concerning religious freedom, in a phrase often echoed in its judgments, the Court affirms that refers it had to take into account "the needs to maintain true religious pluralism, which was inherent to the concept of a democratic society."[20]

Pluralism has to encompass institutions as well as individuals. However, the stress in much modern philosophy and social theory has swung away from the collective and from the social to the individual. It is the nature of so-called liberalism to give priority to protecting the rights of the individual from the perceived coercive force of institutions. Sometimes beliefs and practices as taught by particular religious institutions run against the current norms of wider society. If society intervenes to enforce its own standards, the freedom of institutions to continue existing is put at risk. They cannot remain true to what they conceive of as their own identity. An example was the fate of Catholic adoption societies in England that refused to place children with same-sex couples. They chose to go out of existence rather than conform to new laws. The issue there, as elsewhere, is not whether their stance was admirable or to be condemned. The issue is whether a state can allow institutions to exist that wish to resist prevailing norms. How much difference is to be tolerated, when the differences are motivated by religious differences from the majority?

What happens when, say, views within a religion about the place of women in its organization are at odds with what appear to be the proper ends of sexual equality? Should the Roman Catholic Church be forced to ordain women as priests? When in November 2012 the General

---

20 *Eweida and Others v. The United Kingdom*, Nos 48420/10, 59842/10, 51671/10, and 36516/10, European Court of Human Rights, Judgment, Strasbourg, 15 January 2013, para 73.

Synod of the Church of England voted against particular proposals for accepting women as bishops (though the principle had been accepted), voices were raised in the United Kingdom Parliament suggesting that Parliament should force the Church of England to have women bishops. For Parliament to do so would have gone against the first article of Magna Carta, but for some, the importance of sexual equality had to override all other considerations about the freedom of the church.

This poses a general conundrum about religion and diversity, at an individual and institutional level. Can divergences from norms be tolerated? Complete conformity demands the end not only of a diverse society but of a free one. However, without some agreed standards, there can be no shared institutions and no wider society. The identity of each is challenged. One way of looking at the situation is by thinking in terms of individual consent. We signify our acceptance of the standards of the society of which we are members through our membership in it and participation in its practices. The validity of what is done is constituted by the will of the people in whose name it is done. That may be directly expressed, as in elections, or implied, through continuing membership. Locke puts forward a basic tenet of liberalism when he asserts of every man that, being naturally free, nothing is able "to put him into subjection to any earthly power, but only by his own consent."[21]

If a church or other religious institution wants to maintain its identity, it has to enforce its rules. This approach produced the Spanish Inquisition. Even if such extreme forms of coercion are regarded as immoral, there is still the problem of how can standards be maintained of what is regarded as orthodoxy. The same problem faces all organized religions. Must so-called *sharia* law be enforced on Muslims? There might be agreement that this should not apply to non-Muslims, although that may be controversial in some Islamic countries. A relevant problem is that what *sharia* law should be varies according to the local interpretation of scholars. There is no central Muslim authority such as the Pope and the Vatican for Roman Catholicism.

How far should a religion be allowed to enforce particular standards on those it regards as its members when these standards diverge from those of the society in which the religion is placed? How far should

---

21 "Second Treatise," in Shapiro, *Two Treatises of Government and a Letter Concerning Toleration*, no. 118, p. 152.

the wider society intervene by enforcing its own? There is always the temptation for a majority not to respect the stances of minorities. The Inquisition demonstrated that, but the same dynamic applies if a religion is itself a minority within a society. The underlying issue is how far group rights, as opposed to those of individuals, should be respected. Should an institution, even a religious one, even be able to override the claims of conscience of an individual? Helwys and Williams thought not. However, it is then far from clear that the integrity of any institution can be maintained.

The European Court of Human Rights has stressed that religious institutions are important and that the freedom to leave one is a sufficient safeguard of individual liberty. Religions' integrity must be upheld. In a significant case concerning the right of Romanian priests to form a trade union, in disregard for the discipline of their church, the Court said unequivocally that "in the event of a disagreement over matters of doctrine or organisation between a religious community and one of its members, the individual's freedom of religion is exercised through his freedom to leave the community."[22] This particular case was important, with a significance across Europe, in that it stressed group rights as well as upholding those of individuals. The Court's settled view was firmly expressed when it said, with reference to Article 9 of the European Convention on Human Rights, that "the autonomous existence of religious communities is indispensable for pluralism in a democratic society and is an issue at the very heart of the protection which Article 9 affords."[23] The inner disciplines and understandings of a community have to be respected, it seems, even when they conflict with the wider norms of society. In this case, the widely recognized freedom to form a trade union was not permitted to undermine a church's discipline of its priests. Institutions that are undermined simply by being at odds with the rest of society are then no longer able to continue offering the alternatives that the Court sees as an essential part of democratic pluralism. Needless to say, this principle may arouse difficulties. It is one thing to allow a church to exercise strict discipline over its clergy. There are, though, other cases where religious institutions diverge in

22 Sindicatul "Pastoral Cel Bun" v. Romania, No 2330/09, European Court of Human Rights, Judgment, Strasbourg, 9 July 2013, no. 137.
23 Sindicatul, no. 136.

their practices from the norms of society, as in the case of treatment of women, and many outside the institutions in question may not be willing to be so tolerant.

The demands of diversity, and religious freedom, may suggest that the individual conscience should be of paramount importance. However, without institutions able to provide a clear and consistent message, there is nothing for individuals to choose between. Each person becomes an arbiter of a truth that each has to construct. Given separate institutions, is the sanction of expulsion or excommunication from a religious body an appropriate one? Ordinary sports clubs might feel free to expel unruly members, who hinder the proper functioning of the club. Today, many Catholics object when bishops even suggest such sanctions are appropriate for those who, while claiming to be loyal Catholics, disagree publicly with some major element of Catholic teaching. Catholic politicians advocating same-sex marriage provide one controversial example. Contemporary Protestant churches seem less willing to exercise such discipline, although they used to. The result, however, in some people's eyes, is that such "mainstream" churches seem to preach a message that is progressively more uncertain.

To take the Roman Catholic example again, the problem of doctrinal diversity is a real one. A body that claims to purvey truth cannot speak with too many contradictory voices. However, an authoritarian insistence on one version of the truth appears to attack the very freedom of conscience that even Catholics, since the Second Vatican Council, have claimed to uphold. Like Locke, they have come to recognize the basic God-given freedom of all humans. Certainly the Catholic Church has given up all claim to use the state to enforce its beliefs, as undoubtedly used to happen even in the twentieth century.

What though about its rights over its own members? One Catholic philosopher writes: "the coercive authority of the church, and in particular her authority punitively to enforce obligations to Catholic faith and practice on the baptized, is still fundamental to modern canon law."[24] Such a position can give rise to all kinds of difficulties, some arising from the fact that the practice of infant baptism means that people are regarded as members of the church whether they have consented to be

24 Thomas Pink, "Conscience and Coercion," *First Things*, August/September 2012, p. 46.

or not. Even Protestants are accepted as having had Christian baptism, and it would be hard for the Catholic Church to claim coercive authority over them, if it really believes in freedom of conscience. However, a basic principle of freedom of religion is clear. The ultimate freedom is being able to reject membership of a particular religious institution and leave. In the same way, such an institution has, at some point, to retain a particular right to discipline those who speak in its name, if they appear to be contradicting its core message. A bishop, or even a priest or minister, who publicly proclaims atheism has definitely strayed over a line. Excessive diversity within an institution must undermine it.

Leaving a church, or renouncing a whole religion, may, as the European Court says, be the ultimate guardian of religious freedom, but it has often been prevented in many religious contexts. The liberal ideal of consent and free choice on the part of the individual contradicts the demand that the integrity and identity of institutions and societies be maintained at all costs. The fear, say, of foreign influence through the introduction of alien religions can be all-consuming. In many Islamic countries, for instance, Christianity can be seen as a Western religion. Conversion to it from Islam will not be recognized in law or by society, whatever human rights documents might claim. This can take ludicrous forms, as when Christians are seen in Egypt as Western stooges, despite the fact that Coptic Christianity was established in Egypt centuries before the founding of Islam.

True freedom demands choice. That presupposes the right to choose a religion, to leave one for another, or to adopt none at all. That presupposes the existence of different institutions, which have to maintain the integrity of their message. To revert to the theme of earlier chapters, truth is at stake. We all as humans may, if we are to have genuine freedom, have to face the competing demands of alternative religions, and different versions of the same religion. A truly democratic society will offer such a choice. However, the worry remains that while this may be an inevitable precondition, and result, of the freedom we all possess, such diversity can itself be harmful. It can undermine the whole of a society. Its existence can encourage violence. Indeed, does such competition contribute to the vibrancy of religion, or may it undermine it? That is the issue to which I now turn.

9

RELIGION AS PERSONAL PREFERENCE

RATIONAL CHOICE THEORY

The issue of group rights and individual rights, and the tug-of-war between the doctrinal purity of institutions and the consciences of their individual members, is related to a perennial problem in the philosophy of social science. Is any society simply constituted by individuals and their decisions, or does it have some ongoing collective identity?[1] The question is whether social structures can have independent causal influences on their members or whether the line of cause and effect only goes from the bottom up, from individuals to the organizations they create. Within Christianity, differing doctrines of the nature of the Church or churches, as one mystical body, even the Body of Christ, or a voluntary community or communities, have long theological pedigrees, and have themselves been divisive.

These disagreements reflect controversies about the nature of the relation of the individual and society. Marxism has stressed the social and the collective, with the causal influence of social and economic structures on human lives. Other views see interactions between individuals as the source of social relationships. Many see social relationships in the way economists analyze economic behavior, in terms of rational decisions by individuals about the perceived costs and benefits of certain courses of action. The questionable idea is that people will make decisions only in what they see as in their own interests.[2]

---

1 For a fuller discussion, see Roger Trigg, *Understanding Social Science*, 2nd edition, Blackwell, Oxford, 2001, chapter 3.
2 See Trigg, *Understanding Social Science*, chapter 7.

This has direct relevance to religious diversity, since one current of opinion in social theory sees religious formation exclusively in terms of individual choice, taking economics as its model. Moreover, the economic theory favored is that which tries to analyze the behavior of markets. The idea of the importance of free competition and the free choice of the individual consumer then takes precedence. The argument is that the alleged vitality produced by such competition will give the consumer a better deal. Institutions will then flourish or go under. Diversity is therefore good.

This description is imbued with ideas from the world of capitalist commerce. Given individual free choice, competition will improve the products on offer. Religion is seen as a commodity designed to meet the preferences and desires of various individuals. The notion that people would accept a religion because they believed it to be true is subordinated to the idea of religions having to meet preferences. Paradoxically, the self-serving nature of such preferences is embraced, in contrast to the condemnation of such self-centeredness by many religions. In this model, even my preference for the welfare of others appears important only because it is *my* preference.

These accounts are presumably vulnerable to empirical refutation within social science. Yet they rest on philosophical understandings of the primacy of the individual and the nature of rational choice. The theory is called "rational choice theory," and its view of rationality is its essential feature. The central idea is that there is a "religious marketplace." Individual choice is paramount, and religious diversity is of positive value. Far from religious difference creating division, hostility, and worse, such difference allegedly produces religious vibrancy and health, in contrast to the stultification produced by religious monopoly.

The idea that religion is a personal preference cuts across the relation seen cross-culturally between religion and ideas of identity. I am not who I am because of the kind of soap I use or the car I drive, even though advertisers foster that impression. Religion seems to be a different matter, affecting the way I look at the world and my place in it. Changing one's religion is not something to be entered into lightly. The model of rational choice appears to describe behavior in societies where religion has lost much of its grip and is no longer central to the way life is lived. It could itself be seen as a concomitant of increasing "secularization," the separation of religious influence from society.

An example of the rational choice model comes from the work of sociologists of religion, Rodney Stark and William Bainbridge. They assume that no one religious organization "can offer the full range of religious services for which there is a substantial market demand," and they conclude that "the natural state of the religious economy is pluralism." They therefore assert that "to the extent that religious freedom exists, there will be many organized faiths, each specializing in certain segments of the market."[3] Pursuing their market theme, they point out that this means that there will be an influx of new religions and a withering of old ones, just as firms in a capitalist economy will go bankrupt if they fail to compete, perhaps by continuing to offer old technology.

Stark, in particular, has become identified with this kind of approach.[4] He suggests in a summary of his position that pluralism is the "natural or normal religious state of affairs."[5] There will be attempts to impose religious monopolies, but his claim is that "in the absence of repression, there will be multiple religious organizations."[6] People are different, with different preferences, some wanting more from a religion and some wanting less. He argues that "religious diversity in all societies is rooted in social niches, groups of people sharing particular preferences concerning religious intensity."[7] He supposes that people are "quite similar in their fundamental outlook across societies and history."[8] Rational choice theory will apply cross-culturally and enable us to predict religious vitality and differentiation in the absence of repression.

In a calculation of costs and benefits, some will be prepared to pay high costs and have high involvement, and others will not. Yet all this makes it sound as if religious preferences are fixed, and it is questionable whether that is so. Despite the use of the term "rational," the model redefines ideas of rationality and detaches the process of reasoning from truth. Reason becomes an instrument for finding appropriate means to

---

3 See R. Stark and W. S. Bainbridge, *The Future of Religion*, University of California Press, Berkeley, 1985, p. 108.
4 See Trigg, *Understanding Social Science*, chapter 10 for a fuller discussion of rational choice theory and its philosophical context.
5 Rodney Stark, *For the Glory of God*, Princeton University Press, Princeton, NJ, 2003, p. 17.
6 Stark, *For the Glory of God*, p. 17.
7 Stark, *For the Glory of God*, p. 18.
8 Stark, *For the Glory of God*, p. 18.

given ends. It is not allowed to help establish what the right ends might be.

Stark's basic point is that "given the diversity of religious *demand,* other things being equal, there will be a corresponding diversity in religious *supply:* hence pluralism, the existence of multiple religious organization."[9] This analysis sees religion exclusively in terms of economics. Does a religion give us what we want? The function of religion is to meet the particular tastes and preferences of individuals. The greater the amount of religious diversity, the theory holds, the more chance there is of this happening. If particular desires are not met, new religions, or cults, can fill the gaps. Pluralism is then the lifeblood of the religious marketplace, providing healthy competition and preventing complacency. The idea of religious freedom creating this marketplace for different brands of a religion, or for different religions, to compete for custom has become something of a commonplace, particularly in the context of the United States.

As a thesis in the sociology of religion, this demands empirical support. Is this really what happens? Although rational choice theory is a thesis claiming universal validity concerning religion, its American provenance is striking. It fits well with the views of religion stemming from Thomas Jefferson and James Madison, the third and fourth Presidents of the United States. The model demands the kind of religious freedom they advocated, as they attacked the Establishment of any religion. Both pointed out that any religious monopoly was itself bad for religion, Jefferson in his *Notes on the State of Virginia* remarks on the indolence of its clergy after the government had supported the Church of England for over a century. As a result, he said, "two thirds of the people had become dissenters at the commencement of the present revolution."[10] Madison pursues a similar theme in his "Memorial and Remonstrance," addressing the controversy in post-colonial Virginia over continued financial support for all churches, and not just the Church of England.[11] He welcomed a multiplicity of sects. The

---

9 Stark, *For the Glory of God,* p. 18 (italics in the original).

10 Thomas Jefferson, "Notes on the State of Virginia," *The Separation of Church and State,* ed. Forest Church, Beacon Press, Boston MA, 2004, p. 49.

11 James Madison, "Memorial and Remonstrance Against Religious Assessments," in *The Separation of Church and State,* ed. Forest Church, Beacon Press, Boston MA, 2004, p. 65.

conclusion could only be, it seemed, that, as Jefferson put it, "difference of opinion is advantageous in religion."[12] The multiplicity of sects can act as a check or a balance over all.

Truth is conspicuous by its absence in contemporary discussion about rational choice in religion, and ideas as such do not appear to matter. The thesis is not that competition between alternatives sharpens up and tests claims to truth. The issue is seen purely in terms of answering our preferences, whatever they might be. The essential characteristic of religious belief – that it asserts truths about reality and about our relationship with the divine – slips out of sight. The celebration of religious diversity ignores the difficulty of holding on to any assurance about the truth of one's own religion in the case of constant challenges. Whatever Jefferson may have held about the self-sufficiency of truth, diversity certainly can create psychological difficulties.

Rational choice theory trivializes religion by treating it as a consumer product. It suits an individualist society where all truth is downgraded to "truth for me." The world has to conform to my wishes, not the other way around. Religion becomes a personal and private matter, and not a matter for social concern. If I can believe what I like, or pick and mix whatever bits of whatever religion I choose, it does not seem to matter what I choose. I may, however, go on to reflect that I need not then believe in any religion. Far from being a stimulus to genuine religious vitality, too much competition can end with the repudiation of all religion.

Steve Bruce puts it this way, talking of what he terms the "cancer of choice":

> To the extent that we are free to choose our religion, religion cannot have the power and authority necessary to make it any more than a private leisure activity. Far from creating a world in which religion can thrive, diversity and competition undermine the plausibility of religion.[13]

Freedom to make up our own minds about what the truth is may be one thing, but too much choice can be bewildering. Quite different is the stronger thesis that I am free to choose what the truth shall be for me.

12 Jefferson, "Notes on the State of Virginia," p. 53.
13 Steve Bruce, *Choice and Religion: A Critique of Rational Choice Theory*, Oxford University Press, Oxford, 1999, p. 186.

IS DIVERSITY THE RESULT OF FREEDOM?

Rational choice theory is all of a piece with efforts to see religious belief as the product of individual, and possibly irrational, preference. In a free society, people regularly make such choices, but these choices do not concern issues of public moment. Different people, as consumers, make different choices about, for example, the make of car to drive. The same goes for the choice of religion. This will inevitably lead to an attenuation of the role of religion. It may or may not be important in individual lives, but its importance will depend on the importance that individuals choose to give it, and not on any intrinsic claim it may itself possess. Its public role will be diminished to the point of irrelevance, simply because it has lost its grip on truth. In the words of Steve Bruce, "the road from religion embodied in the great European cathedrals to religion as personal preference and individual choice is a road from more to less religion."[14]

Proponents of the theory may protest. What about, they may say, the comparison between religious pluralism in the United States and the near-monopoly of state religion in Scandinavian countries, such as Denmark? Religion flourishes in the former, and in the latter it looks moribund. Does that not show that monopoly and state recognition and support are stultifying? The conclusion is that competition is good for religion and diversity helps it flourish. That is the quintessential American argument for the separation of church and state, which is seen as an essential element of democracy.

Rational choice theory in religion makes definite, and questionable, philosophical assumptions, but at the same time claims to be an empirical theory giving rise to predictions. In this respect it has a mixed record. Given monotheism, a diversity of religious desires cannot give rise to different deities patronized according to taste. Instead, Stark points out, we will be confronted with "a diversity of *groups*, differing in their approaches to the *same* God."[15] Different denominations arise, making varying demands. An intriguing aspect of this, in the terms expressed in rational choice theory, is that the more "expensive" religious types, demanding high levels of personal commitment and greater

14 Bruce, *Choice and Religion*, p. 7.
15 Stark, *For The Glory of God*, p. 23.

cost, may be attractive to some. The more a religion asks of someone, the more someone may be willing to give, in time, money, and personal behavior.

Forms of religion demanding little may receive little from their adherents. If I pay a large sum of money every year to belong to a sports club, I am more likely to take my membership seriously and use the facilities than I would if the membership fee were nominal. The facilities on offer are likely to be better than those of cheaper competitors. Liberal churches expecting little from their members may even produce a situation where membership seems pointless. They expect little and offer little. At the other extreme, sects demanding total commitment at high cost may be more successful in attracting adherents, if what they offer meets perceived needs.

The basic thesis of rational choice theory is that religious freedom and religious diversity are inextricably entwined. Freedom produces diversity. Monopoly and state control stifle religion. Religious vibrancy in the United States is a result of the freedom of the religious marketplace. Religious decline in Europe is a result of the state establishment of religion. The American separation of church and state allows religion to flourish. All these claims are contestable, even though they can be made even outside the bounds of rational choice theory.[16]

Even the claim that freedom produces diversity is not as obvious as it might appear. Freedom of religion is crucial for anyone who wishes to live a life according to what he or she believes is most important. One cannot function properly as a human being if one is not free to search for what is true, to communicate that truth to others, and to act in accordance with it. If we cannot follow our deep impulses toward religion (or rationally come to the conclusion that they are misleading), we are not truly free. A democracy that simply enforces truth, in accordance with the wishes of the majority, is not a democracy at all. Minorities are ignored and, indeed, suppressed.

Yet the history of fights for religious liberty suggests that diversity is not just a result of freedom. People like Thomas Helwys and Roger Williams, to take just two examples, did not come to their beliefs because of freedom. Their beliefs drove them to demand a freedom that

16 For more on church and state, see chapter 1 of Roger Trigg, *Religion in Public Life*, Oxford University Press, Oxford, 2007.

was sometimes a long time coming. Religious minorities did not originally flourish because they lived in a free society. Their divergence from social norms led them to ask for a freedom of worship, a recognition that society was all too slow to grant. Diversity of religious belief has always been a driving force for greater religious freedom. Similarly, the need for religious freedom has inevitably involved a demand for wider political and economic freedoms. We have already seen how diversity can invite coercion, and that, in reaction, opens up a vision of a greater freedom. Major steps toward religious freedom have always come as a result of existing disagreement and difference. They do not cause either.

The 1689 Act of Toleration in England was a major landmark on the path to freedom. It recognized existing religious dissent and followed a generation after the bitter Civil War, when differences, many of them religious, could no longer be contained. Unrest was never far below the surface after that war until King James II was driven out. The Battle of Sedgemoor in 1685, in Somerset (John Locke's home), itself had marked an unsuccessful uprising against James, in which religious nonconformists played their role. They wanted to put the Protestant Duke of Monmouth on the throne. Resentment had been bubbling since Puritan ministers had been ejected from their parish churches in 1662. Many had been unwilling to accept the Act of Uniformity, imposing the Anglican Book of Common Prayer on all churches. Since then nonconformists, as they were then called, had been consistently harried by the law. Only the advent of King William and Queen Mary brought a greater toleration and official acceptance of religious diversity.

Much the same pattern can be observed a century later in Virginia, where the Church of England was without resident bishops and in the hands of the local gentry. As we saw Jefferson remark, the Church of England had lost its grip on many of the inhabitants, and, as we saw in Chapter 1, the British were championing religious liberty in the colony, giving support for the position of dissenters, in accordance with the Act of Toleration. This was not initially welcomed by defenders of the Church of England in Virginia, but the local elite suddenly found that they needed the support of dissenters in the looming fight with Britain. Some, such as Madison, had a passionate belief in the principle of religious freedom as being at the core of all freedom, but suddenly the demands of dissenters had a political impact that could not be ignored.

The Anglican gentry needed their support. The position is summed up as follows: "At a fundamental level, the development of religious freedom in Virginia was a negotiation in which the political establishment ceded religious liberty in return for support for mobilisation, support the dissenters provided."[17] Yet freedom did not produce religious diversity. A surging diversity claimed a recognition of the dissenters' position that had previously been withheld.

Apart, however, from the exact relation between religious freedom and diversity, rational choice theory contends that a plurality of beliefs and practices is good for religion. It is controversial how moribund the eighteenth-century Church of England was in Virginia before it met challenges from other denominations.[18] There is, however, much to suggest that Anglican religion in the eighteenth century was formal and uninspiring on both sides of the Atlantic. For that reason, among others, Methodism, and the Evangelical Revival generally, arose to wake up the Church of England. Rational choice theory would say that, when needs are not met, competitors will arise to meet them instead.

DIVERSITY AND RELIGIOUS VIGOR

Will greater diversity always be correlated with the flourishing of religion, or will it be a factor that, in the end, tends to undermine all religion? The issue is whether wider choice provides a wider "take-up," because choice provides different things to attract people of different temperaments, or whether the fact of choice sows the seeds of intellectual doubt and competition spawns division and conflict. These are questions with both philosophical and empirical sides. A typical view, which echoes rational choice theory, comes from the philosopher Martha Nussbaum. She writes about Madison's attack on Establishment and on the indolence of clergy:

If we compare the vigor of religion in today's United States, where every sect must compete for adherents, with the weakness and "indolence" of many

---

17 John A. Ragosta, *Wellspring of Liberty: How Virginia's Religious Dissenters Helped Win the American Revolution and Secured Religious Liberty*, Oxford University Press, New York, 2010, p. 166.
18 See John K. Nelson, *A Blessed Company: Parishes, Parsons and Parishioners in Anglican Virginia 1690–1776*, University of North Carolina Press, Chapel Hill, 2001.

of the Established Churches of Europe, which have lost public support over time, we can easily see the truth of his claim.[19]

The contrast is between plurality and vigor, on the one hand, and state recognition, privilege, and perhaps monopoly leading to weakness, on the other. The separation of church and state is thus good for religion, not least because it allows for genuine competition between equals. Therefore, diversity is good. Nussbaum further attacks Establishment by saying: "Knowing you'll get rich no matter what you do is not exactly a recipe for good management or passionate commitment."[20] There are countries where a church's income is guaranteed by the payment of a church tax through the state. That, however, is only one aspect of the Establishment. It is not true of England or Scotland, where the national churches in both countries struggle financially, precisely because they depend on the income from their congregations and have no state support. "Establishment" is a slippery concept and of limited use in any broad sociological comparison.

The comparison between moribund establishments and religion in more pluralist societies animates a sociology of religion that sees religion as matter of consumer choice, stimulated by the provision of alternative possibilities. It coalesces with modern ideas of religion as "spirituality," a word that is all-encompassing in its vagueness. On the one side, it could denote an intense personal relationship with God. It could refer to the life of the greatest saints and mystics, of whatever religion. On the other side, in the contemporary world, the word can become so attenuated that it merely refers to aesthetic experience or artistic expression. It is downgraded, even degraded, from a purported connection with the transcendent to something subjective that is all about me and my particular preferences. Concentrating on such preferences inevitably changes the subject from reality and truth to something different. With a multitude of preferences to be satisfied, given freedom, the inevitable result will be a multitude of religious choices in the marketplace. The "pick 'n' mix" approach in much modern spirituality exemplifies its inherent subjectivism. Religion merely becomes the highly personal matter of what suits each individual.

19 Martha C. Nussbaum, *Liberty of Conscience: In Defense of America's Tradition of Religious Equality*, Basic Books, New York, 2008, p. 95.
20 Nussbaum, *Liberty of Conscience*, p. 95.

This gives a distorted picture of the nature of religion and its characteristic claims about the nature of reality, with an effect on the way we live our lives. Why do other people matter? Religion normally tries to answer that question by putting human life in a much wider, even transcendent context. The costs and benefits of a religious life to the person choosing it are beside the point. A central part of the pluralistic hypothesis of John Hick was that the different "world religions" all agree that salvation or liberation is defined "as the transformation of human existence from self-centredness to Reality-centredness."[21] This does seem to identify an important feature. Bothering about what is in it for me is a serious distortion of the nature of genuine religion. It turns the focus to my own preferences. Instead of my preferences coming to conform with objective obligations of whatever kind, my prime task is then to indulge them as best I can.

Hick's notion of 'the Real' may be too thin, but religions, however they differ, are typically not about what we each severally want. They are about reality, however conceived, and the demands and obligations it places on everyone. Religion cannot be a commodity, like chocolate or cars, tailored to satisfy the whims of consumers. Greater choice can easily produce greater skepticism about the assertions of religion. Rational choice theory is typical of all attempts to privatize religion. By treating religion as being beyond the bounds of reason and as primarily of subjective validity, it ignores or discounts the issue of truth, which we have argued is the very lifeblood of all religion.

Attempts to equate diversity with vigor distort the point of religion, but they also raise issues that can be settled empirically. In England, the existence of considerable religious diversity created the demand for greater toleration in the seventeenth century. The Establishment of the Church of England has never of itself inhibited further diversity. Indeed, a cynic might suppose that it has helped create more diversity. The census of 1851 revealed that nonconformists and Anglicans were more or less equal in number.[22] Yet although there have been times of great religious flourishing in the last two centuries, it cannot be said that in the early twenty-first century, choice entails vigor. The case

---

21 John Hick, *An Interpretation of Religion*, Macmillan Press, London, 1989, p. 303.
22 For a sociological account of religious diversity in Britain, in the context of rational choice theory, see Bruce, *Choice and Religion*.

of Wales is perhaps even more to the point. Far from Establishment stifling competition, the increasing influence of Welsh nonconformity finally brought, at the beginning of the twentieth century, an irresistible demand for the disestablishment of the Anglican Church of Wales. This eventually became a reality in 1920 and was a product of existing diversity. The disestablishment did not provide a stimulus for more diversity or vigor. Despite a proliferation of denominations, Wales is now littered with closed nonconformist chapels and seems a very secular society, compared with fifty or so years ago.

Competition between denominations may even, in the end, have served to blunt their messages and their effectiveness in achieving a wider social influence. Diversity may appear to be a product of vigor for a time, but competition can be at odds with any idea of one truth. This will be exacerbated when not only different versions of the same religion, but different religions compete, and when antireligious world-views are added to the mix. It is even arguable from a sociological standpoint that increasing religious diversity can set a society on a trajectory that leads to it becoming more suspicious of religious claims. That may not be surprising, if, as we have seen, diversity can provide, for some, a philosophical argument for doubt.

"A WALL OF SEPARATION"

Baptists were, from their inception, proponents of the idea of religious liberty. As they were always in a minority, that is perhaps not surprising. The holders of a privileged position are rarely going to object to it and may even take it for granted as part of the natural order of things. Thomas Jefferson, as President of the United States, famously wrote to a Baptist Association in 1801 that, as religion was a matter that lies solely "between a man and his God," it meant "building a wall of separation between church and state."[23] This was his reply to a letter from the Baptists, which itself referred to "America's God."[24] The Baptists wanted a space where all were equally free to adopt their

---

23 Thomas Jefferson, "President Jefferson's reply to Danbury Baptist Association," in *The Separation of Church and State*, ed. Forest Church, Beacon Press, Boston MA, 2004, p. 130.
24 "Letter from Danbury Baptist Association to President Jefferson," in *The Separation of Church and State*, ed. Forest Church, Beacon Press, Boston MA, 2004, p. 129.

own religion, but that did not mean that they were trying to remove all trace of Christianity from wider society.

"A wall of separation" is a phrase that has achieved a life of its own in the American context. It was used by Roger Williams to talk of the gap between "the garden of the Church and the wilderness of the world," although whether Jefferson knew of this is unclear.[25] Martha Nussbaum sums up the general situation when she says: "Religious minorities know what the denial of that separation usually leads to: the imposition of the ways of the majority on all – or at least the public statement that the majority is orthodox, who "we" are, and that the minority are outsiders."[26]

The remedy, it seems to some, is for the public space to be neutral and for all forms of religion to be treated equally. This could mean removing all religion from any possibility of public recognition. One way of being neutral and treating all religion equally is to ignore it all.[27] This kind of policy is reinforced by the philosophical position, seen repeatedly, that religious belief is ultimately irrational. People's idiosyncratic tastes can then be respected only if they do not counter a public policy that has to be derived from sources other than a religious view of the world.

A respect for religious diversity, and the plight of minorities when they confront "orthodoxy," easily becomes a motive for demanding a "secular" view of the state. The separation of church and state then becomes part of that, but it is a complicated notion in itself. It should not only be concerned with "purifying" the state of religious influence. At its best, it is also a principle recognizing that control of religious institutions, or interference with them, by the state is a serious infringement of religious liberty. Interestingly, even the national Church of Scotland, while having a formal relationship with the monarch, has always insisted that the church was in no way the tool of the state, or answerable to it. The queen, or her appointed representative, the Lord High Commissioner, attends the General Assembly, the government of the

25 See John Barry, *Roger Williams and the Creation of the American Soul*, Viking, New York, 2012, p. 307.
26 Nussbaum, *Liberty of Conscience*, p. 15.
27 For more on these themes, see Roger Trigg, *Religion in Public Life: Must Faith Be Privatized?*, Oxford University Press, Oxford 2007, and also Trigg, *Equality, Freedom, and Religion*, Oxford University Press, Oxford, 2012.

church, each year, but symbolically is seated apart from the members of the Assembly as only an observer, albeit an honored one.

What is a secular state? Some British politicians have been known to say with approval that Britain is a "secular democracy." Other politicians have talked of a "militant secularism" at large in the country. The idea of secularity seems to be both welcomed and feared. Different people doubtless mean different things by the term. From a sociological point of view, the increasing diversity of British society, containing adherents of many religions and of none, is at odds with the historical and legal background of the country, which is avowedly Christian. Yet secularism, as a principle, carries with it the further definite idea of driving away all religious contributions to public life.

Some "secular" ideas of the public square prohibit religious ideas from being put forward publicly.[28] The idea of legislators being influenced by their beliefs is anathema, although atheists can apparently let their beliefs motivate them. A public space denuded of religion seems in some "secular" eyes to be fairer. Some are haunted by the idea of a theocracy, where religious authorities, from whatever religion, can claim that they are acting in the name of God and decree the rules of society. The invocation of Islamic *sharia* law in some countries appears like this.

Even in self-proclaimed "secular" societies, secularism comes in many shapes and sizes, some of which are markedly more sympathetic to religion than others are. Their historical contexts shape their attitudes to religion, and the degree of distance they want to keep from it. The secularism of contemporary India, meeting both religious diversity and the influence of Hindu nationalism, is different from that of predominantly Muslim Turkey. Yet both lay claim to the designation. The contrast between France and the United States is particularly striking. Both are Western nations with strong Christian backgrounds. France, however, through its revolution, reacted against the authority of the *ancien régime*, which was bound up with the power of the Roman Catholic Church. The United States was at its founding a predominantly Protestant country, following John Locke's ideas of a theologically grounded religious freedom. The situation has been described succinctly as follows: "Seeking to fashion undivided loyalty to the state and counter

28 See Trigg, *Religion in Public Life.*

the power of the church, French secularism was driven by the desire to protect citizens from religion and not, as in the American case, to also protect religion from the state. The pursuit of liberty stood in opposition to religious freedom, not in collusion with it."[29]

This signals the fact that the separation of church and state can itself be a way of aggrandizing the state. Religious institutions can be left to their own devices, as the private hobbies of individuals. None of them, however, are in a position to challenge the authority of the secular state, however democratically organized. The "people" can aspire to an authority that accepts no rivals. A secular state can be aggressive and threatening to religious people. The atheism of communist countries bore witness to that. Yet that was not secularism, but rather the application of a distinct antireligious worldview. Secular states claim neutrality, and for that reason are favored by liberals favoring individual freedom and even-handedness between all groups and worldviews. For them, secularism goes hand in hand with religious freedom and fairness to minorities in the face of pressure from majorities. That is why diversity can be a driver of secularism.

A SECULAR SOCIETY?

Even though secularism can appear to protect religious minorities, there are dangers in providing equal liberty for all.[30] In distancing itself from all religious beliefs, the state has to treat them all equally, inevitably assuming that none of them can be particular repositories of truth. If any of them were, particular regard should be paid to them. None of them can be regarded as of any importance, other than the fact that they are held and valued by some citizens. Yet because any state has to adopt some principles in deciding what is acceptable behavior, an unflattering view of secularism is that its limits of toleration are whatever the state cannot tolerate. While that could define a totalitarian society, it can also describe the situation in a secular, but democratic, state. Jefferson wrote that "the legitimate powers of government extend

---

29 L. Cady and E. Hurd, "Introduction," in *Comparative Secularisms in a Global Age*, ed. Linell E. Cady and Elizabeth Shakman Hurd, Palgrave Macmillan, New York, 2010, p. 13.

30 For a discussion of the role of equality in the treatment of religion, see Trigg, *Equality, Freedom, and Religion*.

to such acts only that are injurious to others."[31] This is in tune with the liberalism of later writers, such John Stuart Mill, but it assumes too easily that there will be agreement about what is injurious to others. If murder is involved, things are clear-cut. Many of the arguments about religiously inspired practices are, however, precisely arguments about what is harmful or injurious, or how to balance out different harms to different people.

In *On Liberty*, Mill gives the nineteenth-century example of attempts to make Sunday a day of rest for everyone. He says: "Though feeling which breaks out in the repeated attempts to stop railway travelling on Sunday, in the resistance to the opening of museums, and the like, has not the cruelty of the old persecutors, the state of mind indicated by it is fundamentally the same." He sums it up by referring to the notion that "it is one man's duty that another should be religious."[32] His aim is to maximize people's freedom, but there is a flaw in all this. As he himself admits, "the amusement of some is the day's work for others."[33] He seems unconcerned about the fact that some will be forced to work. He remarks that they are not forced to follow those occupations, and so the only objection to Sunday amusements is that they are religiously wrong. His view is that this is something all must decide for themselves.

This is not an arcane example; nowadays, with a seven-day working week being the norm in many forms of employment, the idea that anyone can reasonably object and wish to make Sunday a day of worship is met with the retort that the person so insisting can always change jobs.[34] Yet the freedom to be unemployed is a questionable freedom. The will and practices of the majority begin to set a standard to which all are expected to adhere, regardless of conscience. Far from Sunday rest being imposed on others, as Mill feared, a secular disregard for the religious significance of Sunday itself becomes the norm. People are not expected, as Mill objected, to live in accord with the religious beliefs of others. Instead it seems as if, in a self-consciously secular society, religious people have to live, in public at least, according to the nonreligious, even antireligious standards of others. In a democratic society,

31 Thomas Jefferson, "Notes on the State of Virginia," p. 51.
32 John Stuart Mill, *On Liberty*, ed. J. Gray and G. W. Smith, Routledge, London 1991, p. 105.
33 Mill, *On Liberty*, p. 105.
34 See Trigg, *Religion in Public Life*, pp. 153ff.

where law and practice tend to follow the views of the majority, there may be a reluctance to make exceptions for religious beliefs. They can easily be dismissed as fanatical.

A democratic but secular society may distance itself from religious belief in the name of equal liberty for those of different religions and of no religion at all. Even so, it will follow majority views of what is in the public interest and what should and should not be tolerated. The majority unconcerned about religious principle is bad news for those with religiously formed consciences. The idea of human rights is meant to be a protection for minorities in the face of the tyranny of a majority. The risk is that the small print of the application of rights, such as the right of religious freedom, rests on what the majority finds tolerable. Individuals may be free to have opinions, but restricting their manifestation when they affect others can seem all too reasonable. How are the rights and freedoms of others to be balanced against the demands of an individual's conscience, particularly in the sphere of religion?

Letting freedom of religion trump other rights creates a hierarchy of rights, to the detriment of other rights. However, it is all too easy for those who disagree with the conscientious stand of a religious minority to weigh it in the balance against other rights and find it wanting. The application of human rights can be vulnerable to changes in social attitudes. The fact that religion has been driven from the public sphere and made the object of personal preferences itself devalues its right to be heard or lived by. The preference itself may seem to have no general validity beyond the simple fact that it is held by an individual or a group, which will probably be in the minority. Rowan Williams refers to the influence of secularist rhetoric when he says: "By defining ideological and religious difference as if they were simply issues about individual preference, almost of private 'style,' this discourse effectively denies the seriousness of difference itself."[35] Instead of being arguments about what is true, differences are demoted to irritating facts about awkward individuals and groups, who may be unwilling to fit in with prevailing norms. Public reason then appears to confront mere private prejudice.

The principle that religious claims are incapable of rational discussion allows dangerous views to fester unchallenged. It also allows the state, and its political and legal institutions, to marginalize religion.

35 Rowan Williams, *Faith in the Public Square*, Bloomsbury, London, 2012, p. 26.

It can be seen as the expression of an irrational private prejudice of people who refuse to fit in with what the majority is comfortable with. Religion then becomes something to be managed, controlled, and ultimately ignored. Philosophical issues about the connection of religion with ideas of truth cannot be divorced from the way religion is treated in a society.

Even if a democratic state expresses the will of the people, or at least the will of the majority, resorting to the exercise of unrestrained power must challenge the very freedom that underlies all democracy. Jacques Berlinerblau puts it this way:

The secular vision is statist to the core. In a dispute between the state and religion, the state *always* trumps religion. No matter how orthodox a church might be from its members point of view, the state views this church as equal to all other religious organizations and inferior to the state.[36]

The neutrality of the state toward religion, and its equal treatment of all religious and nonreligious organizations, constitutes secularity. Paradoxically, this also gives the state the power to decide how much to tolerate religion. Religious freedom becomes a gift graciously bestowed on individuals and institutions. It is not theirs by rights. If, however, religious freedom is a human right, as all charters of such rights proclaim, it cannot be granted, modified, or withdrawn for political reasons. Along with other human freedoms, and entwined with them, it lies at the root of democracy. That, however, represents a significant restraint on the power of the state, and even in a democracy, the majority may chafe at it. In a diverse society, the problem of how to make allowances for those with whom we disagree is a pressing one. Does religious diversity present any special case, so that religious freedom is of particular importance? This is a problem to which we must now turn.

36 Jacques Berlinerblau, *How to Be Secular: A Call to Arms for Religious Freedom*, Houghton Mifflin Harcourt, Boston, 2012, p. 15.

FREEDOM AND RELIGION

IS RELIGION SPECIAL?

Should secularists give any special regard to religious views? They are probably glad to see them as personal preferences, to be ranked in democratic society alongside other preferences. Writing from a Canadian perspective, the eminent philosopher and social theorist Charles Taylor argues with a colleague that "respect for the moral equality of individuals and the protection of freedom of conscience and religion" constitute the two major aims of their version of secularism.[1] In other words, secularism ought to have a more positive attitude to the protection of a religious conscience than sometimes seems to be the case. Taylor and Maclure hold up the model of a political society that agrees about basic political principles so we can live together and resolve disputes while accepting differences. They insist the model includes "respect for the plurality of philosophical, religious and moral perspectives adopted by citizens."[2]

Democracy is necessary because of the existence of disagreement, and it needs to respect and, indeed, nourish alternative points of view. There may be different conceptions of a good society, but even if one prevails, others must not be extinguished. That would soon mean the end of democracy. In any democracy, there have to be organized oppositions to government, with opposition parties, which could themselves offer a

---

1 Jocelyn Maclure and Charles Taylor, *Secularism and Freedom of Conscience*, Harvard University Press, Cambridge, MA, 2011, p. 4.
2 Maclure and Taylor, *Secularism and Freedom of Conscience*, p. 5.

plausible alternative. The same goes for any moral or other outlook. We are not omniscient, and we cannot afford to drive away all the views with which we disagree.

Maclure and Taylor see religious diversity as "an aspect of the phenomenon of 'moral pluralism' with which contemporary democracies have to come to terms." They explain moral pluralism in terms of "individuals adopting different and sometimes incompatible value systems and conceptions of the good."[3] As a result, "in the realm of core beliefs and commitments, the state, to be truly everyone's state, must remain 'neutral.'"[4] Indeed, this idea that neutrality helps the identification of everyone with the state runs deep in liberal political philosophy. The idea is that somehow one is a second-class citizen if the state espouses a religious or moral outlook one does not share.

Yet it is a commonplace that in a democracy many citizens are going to deplore things the state does in their name. If a country fights a war to which some, perhaps many, citizens have objections, that does not make it any the less their country. The test is not whether one gets one's way, but whether one is treated as any less a citizen, debarred from some activities or otherwise victimized. My citizenship does not depend on my views being accepted, but rather on my continuing right to offer them freely and to expect them to be taken seriously. A democracy provides an umbrella for disagreement, sheltering everyone. It recognizes difference and should try to accommodate it, but it will never satisfy everyone. Yet it must still have definite policies and pursue them. Democracies cannot allow themselves to be paralyzed by internal dissension.

The idea Maclure and Taylor have is that somehow freedom, neutrality, and the separation of church and state are all bound up together, and that the state, to be fair to everyone, has to be neutral. They regard as indispensable for the operation of secularism "the separation of church and state and the neutrality of the state toward religions."[5] The picture can emerge, if one is not careful, of the state as a neutral referee managing the different and warring preferences of its citizens. Should one type of preference be given any precedence, however? Religion, and morality, can soon appear to have the same weight as any other desire

3 Maclure and Taylor, *Secularism and Freedom of Conscience*, p. 10.
4 Maclure and Taylor, *Secularism and Freedom of Conscience*, p. 13.
5 Maclure and Taylor, *Secularism and Freedom of Conscience*, p. 20.

or wish has. It might seem odd for special provision to be made for the accommodation of some desires and not others.

We saw earlier that religious impulses are built out of very basic elements in human cognition. They are part of what it is to be human, whether we think they are intrinsically reliable or not. Those who wish to deny the significance of such impulses are entitled to do so and should be free to live accordingly. The issue is not, however, whether some people happen to care more about indulging religious preferences than do others. As we have continually argued, the issue concerns beliefs about purported truths, which concern significant questions concerning human destiny. Seeing religion only in terms of preferences and desires can in fact be a deliberate ploy to destroy its significance and possible relevance to others.

To take Mill's example mentioned in the last chapter, if I do not wish to work on a Sunday because I wish to attend public worship, and because of my religious belief that it is a day of rest, should that wish carry more weight than the preference of someone else to take the day off to attend a sporting event? Seen as just preferences, both might matter very much to individuals, and it might be difficult to see why they should be distinguished. Yet human rights law, expressed in the United Nations Universal Declaration of Human Rights and in many national charters, picks out freedom of religion and belief as something that should be upheld, other things being equal. It may be difficult deciding whether other things are equal, but religion must be taken seriously, not just because believers do so, but because of its subject matter.

Conflict can unfortunately arise once different religions are ignored and not given the attention they claim. The fear of religion as an irrational and dangerous force may have its origin in the fact that if religion is the most important feature of someone's life, it cannot be suppressed or ignored without consequences. Democracy should be a system that provides a safety valve for religious tension and religious disagreement, but this means it is not enough for people to believe what they like privately. They must be allowed to bring those beliefs to the public forum and, crucially, to act on them. In a diverse society, not everything can be allowed in the name of religion. Polygamy is a controversial instance of something that may be sanctioned, and even encouraged, in some religions, but which may be forbidden in a democratic society, not least because it may appear to involve injustice to women.

The problem is where to draw the line and decide what can and what cannot be tolerated.[6] Governments and courts can be tempted to draw it narrowly, making freedom of religion and freedom of worship synonymous. Once people are free to attend public worship, it may seem other practices may not be seen as part of the core beliefs of their religion. English courts have been ready to dismiss the wearing of crosses as not required by the Christian religion. Similarly, they have dismissed, as not "core" beliefs, ideas about Sunday observance or beliefs about marriage that have made some reluctant to recognize civil partnerships (let alone gay marriage itself). The European Convention on Human Rights talks of the right to manifest religion or belief "in worship, teaching, practice and observance." Yet it is a matter of contention what counts as practice and observance and how closely it has to be related to the core teaching of a particular religion.

Judgments about what is and is not core inevitably involve courts in theological issues with which they are never competent to cope. Taking evidence on the matter from representatives of a religion will not resolve the matter if some adherents sincerely feel they have an obligation to keep to a stricter interpretation of what is required than do some of the fellow members of their religion, who may feel the representatives do not represent them. Not only can there be diversity between religions in matters of practice; there can be diversity within religions. Most Christians might not find it important to manifest their faith by wearing a cross, but not all would agree. It is evidently the central symbol of Christian faith. Not all Christians observe Sunday in the same way, but some may wish to observe it more strictly, and it is the traditional day for Christian worship.

In a decision about working on Sunday, a British Employment Appeal Tribunal chose to link what is core to what the majority can accept. It relied on a quantitative assessment, about how many people in a group would be affected. If only a few Christians minded working on Sundays, that would suggest a less serious interference with religious freedom than if many did. The Tribunal argued that if a decision

---

6 See Roger Trigg, *Free To Believe? Religious Freedom in a Liberal Society*, Theos Think Tank, London, 2010, and Roger Trigg, *Equality, Freedom and Religion*, Oxford University Press, London, 2012, chapter 8, for more on this complicated topic.

"affected virtually every Christian to a given extent, it would have a greater discriminatory impact than if the same measure affected only a much smaller number of Christians to that extent." In the case in question, the fact that there appeared to be evidence that "many Christians will work on the Sabbath" undermined the claim of those who would not.[7]

The Tribunal seemed happy with assessing numbers to avoid getting involved with theology. When an appreciable number of Christians might be willing to work on Sundays, it is regarded as so much the worse for those who are not. This judgment certainly does not take the issue of conscience seriously. Even when some do not see respect for Sunday as crucial, it may still be of central importance for others. The same reasoning applies to other religions. Many Muslim women do not see the need to wear a headscarf or other forms of distinctive dress, but such a decision does not impinge on the sincerity of those who do. Religions are not internally monolithic. A religious conscience may be informed by the practices of the group, but the practices of a group are also influenced by the consciences of individuals within it. Respecting conscience is as important within any religion as it is in a wider society.

Religious diversity is always a factor even within a religion. In the later judgment of the Court of Appeal in London about Sunday working, Lord Justice Kay said[8]: 'Sensitivity to the diversity of belief between and *within* religions is something which flows from the respect that is accorded to the range of sincerely held beliefs,' He pointed out [9] that reference to a 'core' belief can make a crucial slide between what is perceived core by an individual believer and the core part of a religion as 'objectively' assessed in some way. The latter, indeed, takes any court into theological territory beyond its remit. Despite this legal correction concerning the previous Tribunal's judgment, the appeal was still lost, both for contractual reasons, and because of the interests of the employer. Religious freedom had to take second place to other factors.

---

7 *Mba v London Borough of Merton*, UKEAT/0332/12/SM, Para 46 (United Kingdom Employment Appeal Tribunal, December 13, 2012).
8 *Mba and London Borough of Merton* (2013) EWCA Civ 1562, para 14.
9 *Mba*, para 15.

FREEDOM OF CONSCIENCE?

We are forced back to the question whether conscience is merely a sub-jective matter, or there is something special about a religious conscience. If the former, everything collapses into the idea of strongly held personal preferences. Freedom of religion is lost within the wider notion of free-dom of conscience, and the latter is devalued. Conscience, as such, can then be subordinated to wider interests, such as the interests of employ-ers. Secular interests trump religious ones. Paradoxically, once respect for religious principles is seen as a species of a more general respect for conscience, conscientious stands of a more general kind are more easily dismissed. Freedom of religion implies a more general freedom of con-science, especially the freedom to deny religion. Many serious conscien-tious stands can be respected by analogy with the respect acknowledged due to religion. Yet the more that conscience merely replaces religion, the less specific is the area to be ring-fenced. More practices demand accommodation, and, inevitably, the limitations necessary on accom-modation will grow.

Not all beliefs and preferences can give rise to a ground for reasonable accommodation. We still have to face the problem of which should be ruled out as incompatible with the rights and freedoms of a democratic society. MacClure and Taylor give weight to religion because they see religious commitments as part of a person's moral identity. They claim that "[t]he more a belief is linked to an individual's sense of moral integrity, the more it is a condition for his self-respect, and the stronger must be the legal protection it enjoys." Their conclusion is that "the special legal status of religious beliefs is derived from the role they play in people's moral lives rather than from an assessment of their intrinsic validity."[10] They are trying to allow room in a society, like Canada, where there is now considerable religious diversity, to respect religion, without implying that religion is necessarily about anything important, or that religion deserves special consideration. It is merely that it seems important to individuals as part of their morality.

There is an ambivalence in Canadian courts, we are told by a Canadian professor of law, about whether religious commitment is a

10 Maclure and Taylor, *Secularism and Freedom of Conscience*, p. 76.

"personal choice or judgment made by the individual that is (in theory) revisable," or whether it is to be described as "a central element of the individual's identity."[11] This is crucial in the wider scheme of things, as aspects of identity can be respected but insulated from politics. If, however, religion, as we have argued, necessarily involves judgments about truth, religious claims may become caught up in the give-and-take of politics and not command the respect of the majority. A central element of someone's identity, like gender or race, can be respected, but it has no implications for others. The state can remain neutral about such manifestations. However, once assertions are made about, say, the common good, the issue is no longer one about the believer but about the content of beliefs. Quirks of identity, it seems, can be tolerated. Objections to public policy and demands for opt-outs (for example, when officials in Canada objected to having to register gay marriages) appear to challenge democratic decisions.

MacClure and Taylor conclude that "within the context of contemporary societies marked by moral and religious diversity, it is not religious convictions in themselves that must enjoy a special status but rather, all core beliefs that allow individuals to structure their moral identity."[12] Freedom of religion is a "mere subcategory of freedom of conscience."[13] It all comes down to the intensity of an individual's commitment, and not to what the individual is committed.

The idea that religious principles matter because they express identity avoids knotty questions of truth. Either, then, religious beliefs about truth can be elided into personal preferences, or religion is merely one among many conceptions of public good. Requests for special accommodation for religious principles can be set aside as special pleading. The belief, however, in a transcendent source of obligation not humanly constructed gives religion a special force. The reduction of a claim to objective truth to the one to subjective concern changes the subject in a remarkable way. Caring about something deeply is not the same as the conviction that I am required by some transcendent authority to live in a particular way.

11 Richard Moon, "Freedom of Religion under the Charter of Rights: The Limits of State Neutrality," *UBC Law Review* 45, 2012, p. 499.
12 Maclure and Taylor, *Secularism and Freedom of Conscience*, p. 89.
13 Maclure and Taylor, *Secularism and Freedom of Conscience*, p. 90.

The sense of obligation to a higher authority makes religion frightening to secular proponents of democracy. It suggests an unwillingness to compromise, which is one reason some see religion as intrinsically divisive and in need of stringent control. Yet for a "neutral" state to treat all religious belief as subjective preference is already to decide the issue against the claims of religion. Taking the claims of religion seriously means recognizing they are potentially about more than personal commitments. The idea of religious liberty recognizes that potential. Even if religious liberty is widened to include those who deny religion, making it simply a matter of conscience inevitably downgrades religion. Whether we should treat religion only in terms of individual identity is one of the points at issue in a diverse society.

As we have seen, religion has a collective dimension that makes it particularly vulnerable to manipulation by the state. Its appeal to authorities beyond the state, even to God, endangers other, secular authority. Restrictions on religion, however, will always go to the heart of all freedom, because religion is so central to people's concerns. If I am not free to worship as I wish and to live out my religion more generally, other freedoms are put in question. It is hard to see how I could be politically or economically free if I am not free to advocate my vision of the public good or to make decisions about economic priorities in accordance with religious principles. There is much evidence, both historically and in the contemporary world, that restrictions on religious freedom strike at the heart of all freedoms and can easily give rise to different forms of conflict.[14] People do not readily accept that they are not allowed to live in accordance with their most precious beliefs.

The maintenance of religious liberty, however, ought not to be based on some calculation concerning keeping internal peace, but rather on deep principle. If human rights are to mean anything more than what states find expedient to uphold for a time, they must be grounded in a vision of what it is to flourish as a human being. Our nature includes a propensity to respond in a religious manner to the world and to reason about the significance of such a response. The human wish and ability to hold, reject, or change religious beliefs must be of central importance.

---

14 See Brian J. Grim and Roger Finke, *The Price of Freedom Denied: Religious Persecution and Conflict in the Twenty-First Century*, Cambridge University Press, New York, 2011.

Religious freedom is not the only human right, or the whole of human freedom. What happens when it clashes with other rights? This problem becomes more pressing in a diverse society where there is disagreement about priorities, and a religious minority can find itself at odds with current law. At times of change, social norms also change, and religious majorities can suddenly find themselves as minorities. A relativist will find no difficulty; one must "move with the times." What is right is relative to a given society at a given time. Social attitudes change. Views about, say, the nature of marriage evolve. Such an attitude fits with the view of morality (and religion) as a set of arbitrary preferences, but it does not accord with any idea of human rights. They mean little if they are only what we (whoever "we" are) happen to believe in at a given time. Human rights in a secular society are a bulwark because, given diverse and changing views, they provide a continuing standard by which everything can be judged. In the absence of religion, they themselves even appear to take on a form of transcendental validity.

What happens when rights clash? Religious freedom is often thought fundamental to all freedoms and is often called the "first freedom" in the United States. It is mentioned first in the First Amendment to the Constitution in the Bill of Rights, and many would argue that its position is not a coincidence. Yet even if there can be no hierarchy of rights, the importance of the right to be free in the area of religion, to believe and to manifest our beliefs, does not lessen.

REASONABLE ACCOMMODATION

The diverse, democratic societies of the Western world, however, offer plenty of examples of religion under pressure from the pursuit of other rights. How far should people in a religiously diverse society be expected to modify their practices in the light of the claims of other people who may not agree with them? Majorities in democracies can bear very heavily on the consciences of minorities, and in particular on those of religious people. Professionals in the field of medicine, for example, might be expected to take part in practices, particularly at the beginning and end of lives, they may find repugnant. Freedom is never a matter of merely allowing others to do the things with which you agree. It should be a matter of accepting that others can do things with which we disagree. The idea of freedom and that of diversity are never far apart. As we have argued, democracy must thrive on difference.

One policy might be to try to accommodate difference, even in the course of implementing a policy, instead of riding roughshod over other people's consciences. Canada is an interesting example given that it has been wrestling with issues of religious diversity. One Canadian, describing the situation in Canada in general and in Quebec in particular, from about 2007, writes: "[T]he common language to describe the management or governance of religious diversity became that of reasonable accommodation."[15] The idea was that, if possible, one should make allowances for people's consciences. Like conscientious objectors in time of war, others should not be coerced into going against strongly held principles.

This means that when rights clash, with each other or with public policy, they should be respected as far as is reasonable. Yet this is not always easy, particularly if the state, because of a commitment to imagined neutrality, is itself reluctant to appeal explicitly to any substantive principles.[16] What standards are to be called on to decide what is reasonable? The disputes, which seek resolution, can themselves reappear in arguments about the limits of reason. Religious and nonreligious views have different ideas about standards and what constitutes reasonableness. If all religion is perceived as intrinsically irrational and intractable, the aim of "reasonably" accommodating them becomes problematic. What is to count as "public reason" will itself be highly contested.

At the heart of any idea of reasonable accommodation must be compromise, and in particular, a determination of not coercing a party in a dispute into doing something that seems deeply repugnant. Coercion cuts across ideas of freedom. Yet law itself can coerce, and if a democratic majority ensures a law is passed, what rights should a disaffected minority have not to comply with it, once the law has been democratically discussed and approved? The quick answer seems to be "none" if there is to be one law for all in a society. This is why the prospect of different religious groups living by different laws arouses so much horror. The idea that Muslims or Jews can operate with their own laws

---

15 Lori G. Beaman, ed., "Introduction" in *Reasonable Accommodation: Managing Religious Diversity*, UBC Press, Vancouver, 2012, p. 3.
16 On the neutrality of the democratic state, see Trigg, *Religion in Public Life*, chapter 7.

about marriage, divorce, and so on, outside the agreed framework of a democratic society, begins to undercut the whole idea of democracy. Many would object, for example, if the rights of women under religious laws seemed significantly less than those in force in wider society.

The idea of a society built on different pillars, with each religion forming a different pillar, reminds us of the ruin of an ancient Roman building, when all that is left are the separate pillars alongside each other, with nothing binding them together. The "monolithic" conception of different religions itself can cause problems. Religions themselves can be internally diverse, with different emphases and interpretations. This is apparent in the history of Christianity, but it is also true of other religions. Judaism and Islam have their more conservative wings, as well as other divisions. Courts may find it difficult to assess the validity of someone's stand on religious principle because it might express the view of a minority within a religion. That does not mean an individual's stand is not principled, but within a religion, as well as outside it, majority rule can be oppressive.

RIGHTS IN THE COURTS: AN EXAMPLE

Examples illustrating all this came in cases before the European Court on Human Rights, with judgment given in 2013. They all concerned cases about religious freedom from the United Kingdom. The first one concerned an employee of British Airways wearing a piece of jewelry with a cross against the airline's policy at the time, and the second case involved a nurse in a hospital wearing a cross and chain. Arguments about the public display of symbols often stand as proxy for wider arguments about the whole place of religion in public life. The wider acknowledgment of religious symbols in Russia is a sign of the greater influence of the Russian Orthodox Church. As we have seen, however, the existence of religious diversity, and the importance of not favoring one group over another, may suggest religion should be for private expression and not for public display. In the British Airways case, there was a complication because Sikhs and Muslims were allowed to wear turbans and headscarves, respectively, so the ban on crosses seemed to amount to discrimination against Christians.[17]

---

17 *Eweida*, para 11.

The English courts had held that wearing a cross was not a requirement of the Christian faith in the way, perhaps, that a Sikh's turban
might be viewed as mandatory. Most Christians do not wear crosses.
The submission of the British government summing up the position of
the English courts was as follows: "The applicants' desire to wear a
visible cross or crucifix may have been inspired or motivated by a sincere religious commitment. It was not, however, a recognized religious
practice or requirement of the Christian faith."[18]

The two dissenting judges in the European case commented that a
religion such as Christianity "is not prescriptive" and "allows for many
different ways of manifesting commitment to the religion."[19] The relevant Article of the European Convention on Human Rights, as we
have seen before, refers to the right to manifest one's religion or belief
"in worship, teaching, practice and observance." Such manifestation
can be limited, the next clause asserts, "for the protection of the rights
and freedoms of others." Yet the idea of practice and observance can
become very attenuated and linked simply with ideas of worship. We
have already remarked how there is a perennial temptation for freedom
of religion to be reduced to freedom of worship. Important though
that is, it does not include all obligations of behavior by which a religious person might feel bound. The law may say that unless something is
"required," it may be motivated by religion but is not essential. As in the
case of working on Sundays, the idea of what is required can then be easily defined as what the majority do. Most Christians do not wear crosses,
and so, it seems, crosses are not a necessary manifestation of faith.

Religious practices can sometimes be reasonably overridden by other
considerations. In the case of the nurse, examined by the European
Court, health and safety considerations were regarded as crucial. The
nurse was working on a geriatric ward, and the case suggested that
disoriented patients might grab her cross, or the object might be a
source of cross-infection. Whether these were the main reasons for
the ban on the cross was disputed. The Court, however, felt "hospital
managers were better placed to make decisions about clinical safety

18 *Eweida and Chaplin v United Kingdom*, Application Nos. 48420/10 and 59842/10,
Respondent's Observations para 10.
19 *Eweida*, Joint, partly dissenting, opinion of Judges Bratza and David Thor Bjorgvinsson,
para 9.

than a court."²⁰ In the other case, however, the Court, in a significant ruling, did accept that the desire of the British Airways' employee to manifest her belief "is a fundamental right."²¹ Issues about what other people did were irrelevant. There could be no real dispute about the intrinsic religious significance of a cross. People were capable of having idiosyncratic and unreasonable beliefs, and so mere sincerity might not be enough, but it seemed that, according to European law, genuine religious practice did not have to be uniformly adopted to be recognized as properly springing from a religion, which certainly gave a different emphasis from that given in the English courts.

The economic interests of an employer have often taken precedence over a religious conscience, as in the case of working on a Sunday. Previous judgments of the European Court had taken the view, which we have previously encountered, that freedom of contract is a sufficient guarantee for freedom of religion. If you do not like the requirements of your job, even if they suddenly change, you can always give it up. Such an idea can apply even when the issue is not one of liking, but of being coerced to act against one's religious conscience. Freedom of religion is not in those circumstances being rated very highly, particularly at times of economic difficulty, when other suitable jobs may be hard to come by. In a significant move, the European Court finally backtracked from this insensitive approach in its judgment on the four cases, saying the possibility of changing one's job is only one aspect of the matter to be put in the balance.²²

We have already seen how the European Court of Human Rights treats freedom of religion or belief as one of the foundations of a democratic society, maintaining again in this judgment that "the pluralism, indissociable from a democratic society, depends on it."²³ Following the trajectory of much language about human rights, it also says, "religious freedom is primarily a matter of individual thought and conscience."²⁴ Despite the Court's continued stress in other contexts of the importance of maintaining the nourishing of different institutions, religious

<hr/>

20 *Eweida and others v United Kingdom*, Applications no 48420/10, 59842/10, 51671/10
  1 and 36516/10, para 99, Strasbourg, January 15, 2013.
21 *Eweida*, para 94.
22 *Eweida*, para 83.
23 *Eweida*, para 79.
24 *Eweida*, para 80.

outlooks cannot be overlooked; the familiar tug-of-war between the rights of groups and those of individuals continues to be a problem in issues about law and human rights.

One line often taken, particularly by opponents of all religion, is that the display in a public place of the symbol of only one religion is unfair to the practitioners of another. Letting none of them exhibit their symbols would seem, however, to be merely an example of a secularism that wishes to remove all public manifestation of religion. However, perhaps more important than the use of symbols is the desire of individuals to hold to their consciences and not be forced into behavior they believe is wrong, even when they are in a minority, perhaps a small one. It was in this context that judgment was given on the other two of the four cases under consideration, bundled together by the European Court. Both involved the question of religious freedom balanced against the right not to be discriminated against, in these cases because of sexual orientation.

Rights can conflict, and in one of the cases, a civil registrar, in her position for many years in London, discovered she was expected to register civil partnerships between same-sex couples because of a change in the law. She claimed she could not conscientiously do this because of her Christian beliefs, which were undoubtedly sincere.[25] However, the European Court recalled "that in its case-law . . . it has held that differences in treatment based on sexual orientation require particularly serious reasons by way of justification."[26] The requirement that freedom of religion be limited by consideration of the rights and freedoms of others meant that the right to manifest her beliefs was "trumped" by the right not to suffer discrimination. Given that in a democratic society, arbitrary discrimination on such grounds as race, and, in this case, sexual orientation is regarded as a breach of individual equality and dignity, the question is how far such a thing is reasonable.

This brings us back to the issue of reasonable accommodation. When two recognized rights conflict, making no effort to accommodate each does not take seriously the needs of a diverse society, with diverse religious views. Many may think the civil registrar is behaving unreasonably, and that she should give up her job if she refuses to apply

25 For more on the *Ladele* case, see Trigg, *Equality, Freedom and Religion*, p. 93ff.
26 *Eweida*, para 105.

the law as it now stands. There must, it would be said, be only one law for all, and "reasonable accommodation" does not involve helping those who are unreasonable. The idea of equality must be at the root of democracy and must not be watered down in some compromise. From the Canadian context, it has been alleged that "reasonable accommodation renders the response to difference as one of benevolence rather than a right to equality."[27] It assumes a condescension by the majority to a minority.

Yet, regardless of who is in the majority, accommodation should not be regarded as a majority graciously tolerating a minority, and perhaps only within limits set by the majority. Genuine accommodation should be a mutual transaction whereby each recognizes the intrinsic rights of the other and tries to ensure that, within reason, they are addressed. Article 14 of the European Convention on Human Rights explicitly gives religion as one of the prohibited grounds of discrimination, so the demands of equality and fair treatment might suggest that religious conviction should be respected as much as race, gender, sexual orientation, and other such grounds. The whole language of equal rights suggests that rights are not the gift of a majority, with exemptions to law in their gift. Rights are built into the scheme of things, should be recognized, and in cases of clashes, a reasonable balance achieved between them. Only in that way can minorities, particularly religious ones, gain protection in a secular society. Power structures vary, but the temptation in a democracy is always to make prevailing public opinion the final arbiter. In the interests of justice for all, this temptation must be resisted.

Such a balance of rights can easily be made in a "reasonable" way. A Muslim who takes on a job as a bartender and then refuses to serve alcohol is being unreasonable. A supermarket that insists on putting a Muslim employee in charge of alcohol provision when there are many other roles to be filled is also being unreasonable. Religious concerns, however, are often subordinated to other social priorities in European courts. The test of a truly free and diverse society must be that people are allowed to live according to their most basic principles, even when these principles diverge from conventional opinion. Freedom only exists when we are willing to allow others to act in ways with which we disagree.

27 Lori G. Beaman, ed., "Conclusion" in *Reasonable Accommodation*, 218.

THE PUBLIC GOOD

If we dismiss issues of truth, particularly in connection with religion, we can easily take it for granted that people's dignity is expressed through their own choices. They are, in a Nietzschean fashion, self-creating beings, whose lives, like artists' canvases, possess the meaning each gives it, for whatever reason.[28] Differences ought to be respected simply as part of the intrinsic dignity each human has. The connection with a stress on respecting individual preferences is obvious. Yet the view is incoherent because it stems from a stress on the objective dignity of human beings and our need to respect it. Some would hold that the idea of human worth has itself a clear religious origin: for example, that we are all made in the image of God. If that might be so, dismissing religion or seeing it only as a subjective preference may well be risky as it undermines a reason many have for believing in human dignity in the first place.

The stress on the ultimate value of each atomistic individual, although itself needing justification, fails to meet the conundrum of how we live together in any society and how we balance all the choices when they conflict with each other. Some notion of the common good is needed. One method is to aggregate preferences in a democratic way, and to let the majority get their way, imposing their will on minorities. Most might then get what they want, but even then, a reasonable accommodation may better enable both majorities and minorities to achieve their ends. That method, however, brings us back to the question not just of what people want, but of how what is good for everyone can be achieved.

Democratic societies, encompassing major disagreement about priorities, cannot escape the issue of the weight, if any, to be given to religious convictions. While religious people must not coerce those who disagree, but rather maximize freedom, secularists have to acknowledge the existence of a religious conscience. They should consider whether legal exemptions might be made in particular cases. Yet there is a very real fear that society will splinter unless one law is rigorously applied to all. The words of John Locke, in making a distinction between the

---

28 For more on Nietzsche's views, see Roger Trigg, *Ideas of Human Nature*, 2nd ed., Basil Blackwell, London, 1999, chapter 10.

role of the "magistrate" and that of conscience, have been influential, not least among the American Founders.[29] Locke said, "The private judgment of any person concerning a law enacted in political matters, for the public good, does not take away the obligation of that law, nor deserve a dispensation."[30] However, such a statement does not seem to meet the concerns of those who are not merely in a political minority, but who have deep objections (of a religious or antireligious kind) to having to obey a law they view as immoral, stemming from their understanding of the nature of human life.

Exceptions are made in many countries in favor of conscientious objection in time of war. Problems arise in modern medicine: Might future doctors and nurses be required to practice euthanasia or to participate in assisted suicides if those practices become legal? All those cases involve beliefs about the sanctity of human life, which lie at the heart of much religion. Locke certainly had to contend with different understandings of Christianity, but it is more complicated when Christian beliefs – or, indeed, the basic precepts of any religion – are challenged. The law may appear to coerce people into taking part in practices that go against everything they hold dear.

The problem lies in Locke's reference to "the public good." Issues of principle do not arise when individuals put private interest before public good. They are merely being selfish. The difficulty is adjudicating between rival conceptions of what constitutes public good. Imposing one conception of it in a uniform manner is the stuff of totalitarianism. Religions are particularly likely to have deep-rooted conceptions of the common good. They will have a clear idea of what constitutes human flourishing, and their ideas may well differ from each other and from more secular ideas. In pluralist societies, where diversity is the norm, the aim must be not only to resolve disputes but to resolve them in ways that leave the integrity and outlook of different groups intact. "Multiculturalism" all too often becomes a relativism that isolates communities instead of drawing them into a debate of where the common good may lie. Different conceptions of the public good are not ends in themselves. Diversity of belief should not so much be celebrated as be

29 See, for example, Vincent Phillip Munoz, *God and the Founders*, Cambridge University Press, New York, 2009.
30 Shapiro, ed., "A Letter Concerning Toleration" in *Two Treatises*, 243.

something with which we are engaged and through which we work. There is still an issue as to what is right. Even so, concern for minority views should be the very stuff of democracy.

Each state has to have definite principles, not the least of which is an affirmation of the dependence of democracy on notions of equality and freedom. A society formed by Christian principles, or those of some other religion, need not give those up in the interests of pluralism. The issue is what welcome is given to alternative beliefs, and the freedom with which they can, within reasonable limits, be put into practice. A free society must treat its citizens equally, not picking out some for special favor. It will be inconsistent, for example, to allow the wearing of a Muslim headscarf but not a Christian cross. A belief in equality, however, has to be grounded. It is not a substitute for definite belief, but it is itself a substantive one of great importance, containing important insights into a constituent part of the public good. Inevitably those insights may be bound up with religious views.

Religious people have views about the common good and should be allowed to express them and live by them as far as is possible. Religion is not merely a central part of the lives of individuals. It makes crucial claims about the nature of a good society. The view of religion as an irrational preference may make it appear less significant, but it distorts its nature in denying that it typically makes truth claims, affecting our understanding of human nature and the place of humans in society. Religion has a political relevance, not only because it creates problems in divided societies but also because it can contribute to public debate concerning what constitutes human welfare and harm. Even if some forms of religion can be harmful, involving them in public debate will help expose this.[31] The alternative is to allow them to fester unseen and unchallenged. When controversial issues are at stake, simply impos-ing one view or set of practices on those who differ stifles democratic freedom. All societies need basic animating principles, but the belief in freedom has to be basic. However, such a belief itself depends on the alleged truth of certain beliefs about the human condition. It itself

31 On the vexed issue of what limits there should be to religious freedom, and where lines should be drawn on what is to be permitted, see *Free to Believe? Religious Freedom in a Liberal Society*, Theos Think Tank Report, London, 2010, and also *Equality, Freedom and Religion*, Oxford University Press, New York, 2012.

assumes the possibility of objective truth, and is often closely linked, as in the philosophy of John Locke with religious views. He holds that "God having given man an understanding to direct his actions, has allowed him a freedom of the will, and liberty of acting."[32]

For political reasons, the First Article of the Universal Declaration of Human Rights does not mention God, but the religious provenance at the outset is clear. We read: "All human beings are born free and equal in dignity and rights. They are endowed with reason and conscience and should act towards one another in a spirit of brotherhood." The idea of brotherhood implicitly invokes the idea of a common Father, a Creator who is the source of our nature (and is invoked explicitly in the American Declaration of Independence). One does not have to be religious to accept this view of a natural law, but it helps.

Any democracy that wants to uphold the values expressed in the Declaration, as it should, attacks manifestations of a religious conscience at its peril. Such a conscience provides a justification for belief in them. The human freedom that gives rise to such diversity of belief and practice should be cherished. Along with the exercise of reason, it is essential for understanding what is true. Freedom, reason, and the idea of truth are all indissolubly linked. Remove one and all else falls. None of us may possess as much of objective truth as we would like, and this gives rise to diversity and disagreement. The limitations of being human are all too obvious, but striving for truth, in many spheres, remains our most important characteristic. That situation leaves us with an undoubted conundrum. Diverse beliefs, often in disagreement with each other, are a challenge from an intellectual and political standpoint, particularly in the area of religion where the most difficult, and intractable, issues are faced by humans trapped in finitude. We must engage with those disagreements. Merely accepting them, or "celebrating" them, is to fail to take them seriously. However, the imposition, through coercion, of one set of opinions and practices also fails to respect the freedom, reason, and yearning for truth that should underlie all religion.

---

32 Locke, Second Treatise, #58, 124.

BIBLIOGRAPHY

Ayer, A. J. *Language, Truth and Logic*, Victor Gollancz, 2nd ed. London 1946.

Barrett, J. *Why Should Anyone Believe in God?* Alta Mira Press, Lanham, MD 2004.

Barrett, J. *Cognitive Science, Religion, and Theology: From Human Minds to Divine Minds*, Templeton Press, West Conshohocken, PA 2011.

Barry, J. *Roger Williams and the Creation of the American Soul*, Viking, New York 2012.

Beamen, L. F. *Reasonable Accommodation: Managing Religious Diversity*, UBC Press, Vancouver 2012.

Berger, P. and Zijderveld, A. *In Praise of Doubt: How to Have Convictions Without Becoming a Fanatic*, HarperOne, New York 2009.

Berlinerblau, J. *How to be Secular: A Call to Arms for Religious Freedom*, Houghton, Mifflin Harcourt, Boston 2012.

Bethencourt, F. *The Inquisition: A Global History, 1478–1834*, Cambridge University Press, Cambridge 2009.

Biggar, N. and Hogan, L. *Religious Voices in Public Places*, Oxford University Press, Oxford 2009.

Bloom, P. *Descartes' Baby: How the Science of Child Development Explains What Makes Us Human*, Arrow Books, London 2005.

Bruce, S. *Choice and Religion: A Critique of Rational Choice Theory*, Oxford University Press, Oxford 1999.

Bruce, S. "The Social Process of Secularization," *Blackwell Companion to Sociology of Religion*, ed. Fenn, R. K., Blackwell, Oxford 2001.

Cady, L. E. and Hurd, E. S. *Comparative Secularisms in a Global Age*, Palgrave Macmillan, New York 2010.

Castelli, M. "Faith Dialogue as a Pedagogy for a Post-Secular Religious Education," *Journal of Beliefs and Values* 13, 2012.

Cavanaugh, W. *The Myth of Religious Violence*, Oxford University Press, New York 2009.

Chater, M. and Erricker, C. *Does Religious Education Have a Future?* Routledge, London 2013.

Church, F. (ed.). *The Separation of Church and State: Writings on a Fundamental Freedom by America's Founders*, Beacon Press, Boston 2004.

Cohen, E. *The Mind Possessed: The Cognition of Spirit Possession in an Afro-Brazilian Religious Tradition*, Oxford University Press, Oxford 2005.

Cottingham, J. *The Spiritual Dimension: Religion, Philosophy, and Human Value*, Cambridge University Press, Cambridge 2005.

Dawkins, R. *The God Delusion*, Bantam Press, London 2006.

Eweida and Others v. United Kingdom, Nos 48420/10, 59842/10, 51671/10 and 36516/10 European Court of Human Rights, Strasbourg 13 January 2013.

Folgero v. Norway, Grand Chamber, European Court of Human Rights, Strasbourg, No 15472/02, 29th June 2007.

Gregory, B. *The Unintended Reformation: How a Religious Revolution Secularized Society*, Belknap Press, Harvard University Press, Cambridge, MA 2012.

Grim, B. and Finke, R. *The Price of Freedom Denied: Religious Conflict and Persecution in the Twenty-first Century*, Cambridge University Press, New York 2011.

Hallett, G. *One God of All? Probing Pluralist Identities*, Continuum, New York 2010.

Helwys, T. *A Short Declaration of the Mystery of Iniquity*, ed. Mercer, R. Groves, University Press, Macon, GA 1998.

Hick, J. (ed.). *The Myth of God Incarnate*, SCM Press, London 1977.

Hick, J. *An Interpretation of Religion: Human Responses to the Transcendent*, Macmillan, Basingstoke 1989.

Hick, J. "An Irenaean Theodicy," *Encountering Evil*, ed. Davis, Stephen T., Westminster John Knox Press, Louisville, KY 2001.

Hosanna-Tabor Evangelical Lutheran Church and School v. Employment Opportunity Commission, 132 S. Ct. 694 (2012) (Alito J. concurring).

Kelemen, D. "Are Children 'Intuitive Theists'?" *Psychological Science* 15, 2004.

Kuhn, T. S. *The Structure of Scientific Revolutions*, University of Chicago Press, Chicago 1962.

Kuhn, T. S. "Reflections on my Critics," *Criticism and the Growth of Knowledge*, ed. Lakatos, I. and Musgrave, A. Cambridge University Press, Cambridge 1970.

Leiter, B. *Why Tolerate Religion?* Princeton University Press, Princeton, NJ 2012.

Laïcité et République, Rapport au President de la Republique, La Documentation Francaise, Paris 2004.

Locke, J. *Essay Concerning Human Understanding*, ed. and abridged by Pattison, A. S. Pringle, Oxford University Press, Oxford 1924.

Locke, J. *Political Essays*, ed. Goldie M., Cambridge University Press, Cambridge 1997.

Locke, J. *The Reasonableness of Christianity*, reprinted from 1794 ed. (originally published 1695), Thoemmes Press, Bristol 1997.

Locke, J. *Two Treatises of Government and A Letter Concerning Toleration*, ed. Shapiro, I., Yale University Press, New Haven, CT 2003.

Maclure, J. and Taylor, C. *Secularism and Freedom of Conscience*, Harvard University Press, Cambridge, MA 2011.

Mba v. London Borough of Merton (United Kingdom Employment Appeal Tribunal) (2012) UKEAT/0332/12/1312.

McCauley, R. N. *Why Religion Is Natural and Science Is Not*, Oxford University Press, New York 2011.

Mcfarlane v. Relate Ltd (Court of Appeal, London) EWCA civ B1, 2010.

McKim, R. *Religious Ambiguity and Religious Diversity*, Oxford University Press, New York 2001.

McKim, R. *On Religious Diversity*, Oxford University Press, New York 2012.

Mill, J. *On Liberty*, ed. Grey, J. and Smith, G. W., Routledge, London 1991.

Miller, N. P. *The Religious Roots of the First Amendment: Dissenting Protestants and the Separation of Church and State*, Oxford University Press, New York 2012.

Mitchell, B. (ed.). *The Philosophy of Religion*, Oxford University Press, Oxford 1971.

Moon, R. "Freedom of Religion under the Charter of Rights: The Limits of State Neutrality," *UBC Law Review* 45, 2012.

Munoz, V. P. *God and the Founders: Madison, Washington, and Jefferson*, Cambridge University Press, New York 2009.

Nelson, J. K. *A Blessed Company: Parishes, Parsons, and Parishioners in Anglican Virginia 1690–1776*, University of North Carolina Press, Chapel Hill 2001.

Nussbaum, M. *Liberty of Conscience: In Defense of America's Tradition of Religious Equality*, Basic Books, New York 2008.

Nussbaum, M. *The New Religious Intolerance: Overcoming the Politics of Fear in an Anxious Age*, Belknap, Harvard University Press, Cambridge, MA 2012.

O'Collins, G. *Salvation for All: God's Other Peoples*, Oxford University Press, Oxford 2008.

Pera, M. *Why We Should Call Ourselves Christians: The Religious Roots of Free Societies*, Encounter Books, New York 2008.

Peterson, M. D. and Vaughan, R. C. (ed.). *The Virginia Statute for Religious Freedom: Its Evolution and Consequences in American History*, Cambridge University Press, Cambridge 1988.

Phillips, D. Z. *The Concept of Prayer*, Routledge and Kegan Paul, London 1965.

Phillips, D. Z. *Death and Immortality*, Macmillan, London 1970.

Phillips, D. Z. *Wittgenstein and Religion*, Macmillan, Basingstoke 1993.

Pincus, S. *1688: The First Modern Revolution*, Yale University Press, New Haven, CT 2009.

Pink, T. "Consciousness and Coercion," *First Things*, August–September 2012.

Plantinga, A. *Warranted Christian Belief*, Oxford University Press, New York 2000.

Popper, K. *Objective Knowledge: An Evolutionary Approach*, Oxford University Press, Oxford 1972.

Quebec v. Loyola High School (Quebec Court of Appeal) 2012 QCCA 2139.

R v. JFS (United Kingdom Supreme Court) UKSC 15, 2009.

Ragosta, J. A. *Wellspring of Liberty: How Virginia's Dissenters Helped Win the American Revolution and Secured Religious Liberty*, Oxford University Press, New York 2010.

Ratzinger, J. *Truth and Tolerance: Christian Belief and World Religions*, Ignatius Press, San Francisco 2004.

Runzo, J. (ed.). *Is God Real?* Macmillan, Basingstoke 1993.

Rossiter, C. (ed.). *The Federalist Papers*, Signet Classic, New York 2003.

S.L et al v. Commission Scolaire des Chenes et al. (Supreme Court of Canada) 2012 SCC7 and 426 N.R. 2012.

Shortt, R. *Christianophobia: A Faith under Attack*, Random House, London 2012.

Sindicatul 'Pastorul Cel Bun' v. Romania, No 2330/09, European Court of Human Rights, Strasbourg, 9 July 2013.

Stark, R. *For the Glory of God: How Monotheism Led to Reformations, Science, Witch-Hunts, and the End of Slavery*, Princeton University Press, Princeton NJ 2003.

Stark, R. and Bainbridge, W. S. *The Future of Religion: Secularization, Revival, and Cult Formation,* University of California Press, Berkeley 1985.

Taliaferro C., and Teply, A.J. (ed.). *Cambridge Platonist Spirituality,* Paulist Press, New York 2004.

Tillich, P. *The Shaking of the Foundations,* Charles Scribner's Sons, New York 1948.

Tillich, P. *Dynamics of Faith,* Harper and Row, New York 1957.

Toledo Guiding Principles in Teaching about Religions and Beliefs in Public Schools, OSCE (Organisation for Security and Cooperation in Europe), 2007.

Trigg, R. *Reason and Commitment,* Cambridge University Press, Cambridge 1973.

Trigg, R. *The Shaping of Man: Philosophical Aspects of Sociobiology,* Blackwell, Oxford 1982.

Trigg, R. *Reality at Risk: A Defence of Realism in Philosophy and the Sciences,* 2nd ed., Hemel, Hempstead 1989.

Trigg, R. *Rationality and Science: Can Science Explain Everything?* Blackwell, Oxford 1993.

Trigg, R. *Rationality and Religion: Does Faith Need Reason?* Blackwell, Oxford 1998.

Trigg, R. *Ideas of Human Nature: An Historical Introduction,* 2nd ed., Blackwell, Oxford 1999.

Trigg R. *Understanding Social Science: A Philosophical Introduction to the Social Sciences,* 2nd ed., Blackwell, Oxford 2001.

Trigg, R. *Morality Matters,* Blackwell, Oxford 2005.

Trigg, R. *Religion in Public Life: Must Faith be Privatized?* Oxford University Press, Oxford 2007.

Trigg, R. *Free to Believe? Religious Freedom in a Liberal Society,* Theos Think Tank, London 2010.

Trigg, R. *Equality, Freedom, and Religion,* Oxford University Press, Oxford 2012.

Vattimo, G. *A Farewell to Truth,* Columbia University Press, New York 2011.

Williams, R. *Faith in the Public Square,* Bloomsbury, London 2012.

Wilson, E. O. *On Human Nature,* Harvard University Press, Cambridge, MA 1978.

Wilson, E. O. *The Social Conquest of Earth,* Liveright Publishing Corporation, New York 2012.

Wittgenstein, L. *Philosophical Investigations,* trans. Anscombe, G. E. M., Blackwell, Oxford 1958.

Wittgenstein, L. *On Certainty*, ed. Anscombe, G. E. M. and von Wright, G. H., Blackwell, Oxford 1969.

Wittgenstein, L. *Lectures and Conversations on Aesthetics, Psychology and Religious Belief*, ed. Barrett, Cyril, Blackwell, Oxford 1966.

Wittgenstein, L. *Remarks on Frazer's "Golden Bough"*, ed. Rhees, Rush, Brynmill, Retford 1979.

INDEX